Critiques of Pure Abstraction

Mark Rosenthal, Guest Curator

A traveling exhibition organized and circulated by Independent Curators Incorporated, New York

Critiques of Pure Abstraction is sponsored by

PHILIP MORRIS COMPANIES INC.

The exhibition is also supported by grants from the National
Endowment for the Arts and the Foundation-To-Life, Inc.,
with additional funding from the ICI International Associates.

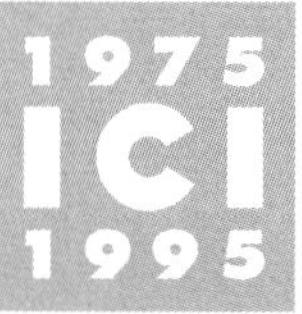

Itinerary

Sarah Campbell Blaffer Gallery
University of Houston
Houston, Texas
January 28–March 26, 1995

Illingworth Kerr Gallery
Alberta College of Art
Calgary, Alberta, Canada
August 17–October 14, 1995

Sheldon Memorial Art Gallery
University of Nebraska
Lincoln, Nebraska
November 7, 1995–January 7, 1996

*UCLA at the Armand Hammer
Museum of Art and Cultural Center*
Los Angeles, California
January 30–March 10, 1996

Crocker Art Museum
Sacramento, California
March 29–May 5, 1996

The Lowe Museum
University of Miami
Coral Gables, Florida
September 19–November 17, 1996

Frederick R. Weisman Museum
University of Minnesota
Minneapolis, Minnesota
April 3–June 15, 1997

Acknowledgments   As we near the end of this decade, it seems particularly appropriate to view the work of artists who both examine and participate in the trajectory of Abstraction, a movement that began in the early part of this century. I was delighted when Mark Rosenthal agreed to curate this exhibition for ICI, and I am grateful for his gracious curatorial diligence, his persistent efforts throughout the long process of bringing the exhibition into existence, and for his thoughtful catalogue essay.

The combined efforts of ICI's staff—Judith Olch Richards, Jack Coyle, Lyn Freeman, Virginia H. Strull, Alyssa Sachar, Heather Glenn Junker, and Stephanie Spalding—have made this exhibition, and all that ICI accomplishes, possible. My gratitude to each of them, and to Jeanne Breitbart, Hitomi Iwasaki, and Anne Longnecker, is boundless.

The generous support of Philip Morris Companies Inc., as the sponsor of this exhibition, is deeply appreciated—as is the additional support of the National Endowment for the Arts, the Foundation-to-Life, Inc., and the ICI International Associates for this project in ICI's 20th anniversary year. I would also like to acknowledge and thank all the members of ICI's Board of Trustees for their active involvement and support of our exhibition program; their commitment infuses each of ICI's exhibitions.

Susan Sollins
Executive Director

Critiques of Pure Abstraction   by Mark Rosenthal

It is remarkable to observe, as the end of the 20th century approaches, that the practice of pure abstraction, which has spanned almost the entire century, continues even now to attract new adherents. Pioneered in the second decade of the century by the painters Wassily Kandinsky, Kasimir Malevich, and Piet Mondrian as a mode in which there appeared to be no referents to the world of appearances, abstraction spread throughout Europe and the United States, influencing generations of painters and sculptors, as well as architects and designers who also made use of simple geometric forms and broad expanses of uninflected color. Abstraction's visual purity—the absence of signs of anecdotal life—was often accompanied by notions of spirituality and lofty idealism. During the first third of the century it was the chosen style of utopianist social movements; in the postwar years, in the United States, abstraction was considered a vehicle for personal liberation.

The longevity of abstraction, and its survival as a viable option in the face of multitudinous, competing aesthetic thrusts, has made it virtually ubiquitous as a sign of the modern period. But many contemporary artists have embraced an approach that steps beyond the premises that have dominated the modern period of the 20th century. Their approach, the postmodern outlook, skeptically examines the issues of the preceding period. Abstraction, as a totem of modernity, has become a favorite subject of such examination, with its "character"—its apparent purity and self importance—being called into question. In so many words and pictures, abstraction has been made to appear superficial, unaccommodating of various social concerns, or anachronistic in the

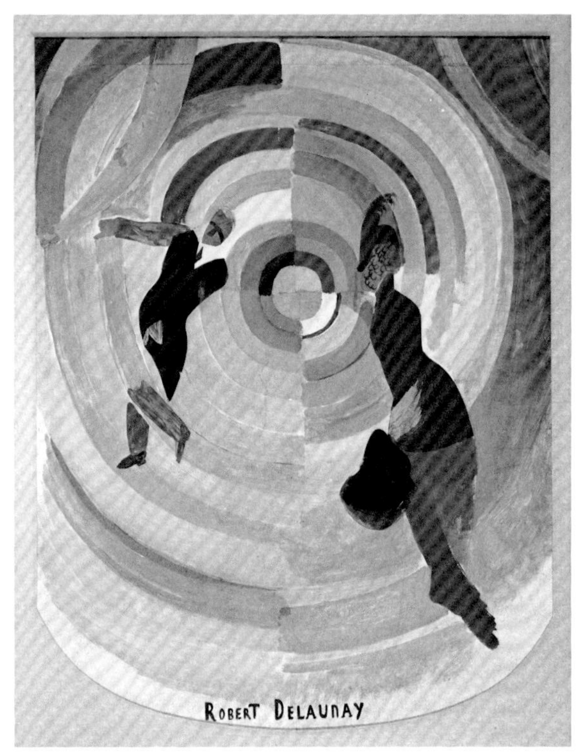

FIG. 1 Robert Delaunay
Political Drama, 1914. Oil and collage on cardboard, 35 × 26 inches. Gift of the Jospeh H. Hazen Foundation, Inc. ©1994 Board of Trustees, National Gallery of Art, Washington, DC

postmodern world. For the sake of argument, I have joined all of these attitudes together, calling them "critiques."

This exhibition includes a sampling of artists. Some practice pure abstraction but seek to reform it so as to be responsive to contemporary issues; some mock the style as if it were antiquated and senile; others investigate its basic nature. These artists' works offer a dialogue with abstraction as well as a criticism, and both contexts are important to an understanding of them. While the tendency to debate abstraction has grown through the 1980s and 1990s to occupy a considerable corner of contemporary art, this contrarian view was evolving along with uncritical work well before 1980. Therefore, to enlarge the chronological framework, this exhibition includes a few of the relatively recent forerunners. Nevertheless, it should be noted that abstraction and questions about its validity have been under attack since the decade of its birth.

Abstraction was a mere stageset for figurative events in both Robert Delaunay's *Political Drama* (1914) (fig. 1) and Marc Chagall's *The Traveller (Forward!)* (1919–20). These works at once explored the place of the human being in an abstract world, and responded to this inquiry by suggesting a foreground-background relationship. In Russia, Ivan Puni was even more blunt, placing an actual hammer in a painted abstract milieu (*Still Life: Relief with Hammer,* 1915/17), thereby asserting that the human artifact would always have a dominating and "real" existence compared to the artful, non-referential composition. In 1921, Alexander Rodchenko demonstrated that the course of pure abstraction was fated to conclude with a trio of monochrome canvases; these were included as part of an exhibition balefully entitled *The End of Painting.* That such works were made early in the century indicates that abstraction did not enter the world in an uncontested fashion but, rather, that because it was so heralded by its chief adherents this style was almost immediately subject to scrutiny.

During the 1950s, even as American Abstract Expressionism dominated the artistic stage, critiques multiplied, with abstraction being systematically undercut, deconstructed, and referenced as if it belonged to a past world. In an antic spirit, Robert Rauschenberg painted bland monochromes in the early 1950s, while Ad Reinhardt, Joseph Albers, Mark Rothko, and Barnett Newman seriously examined the permutations of this principal abstract strategy. Rauschenberg challenged whether the Abstract Expressionists' "Nothing," a subject matter of great portent, still deserved to be capitalized; for him it was merely nothing, a Cagean sponge in the everyday world of appearances. Jasper Johns's *Green Target* (1956) showed that the timeless world of the monochrome could contain something altogether transitory, a flat bed of newsprint carrying the events of the day. Instead of being out of time as much classic abstract art presumed, Johns's abstraction belonged to a specific place in time. That same year, Nam June Paik installed Barnett Newman's apparently sacred "zip" in the context of the modern world. Amidst a sea of televised static, the "zip" was now afloat and adrift. Whereas Newman's line was intended to have a metaphysical meaning in his canvases, suggesting God's name with titles such as *Onement*, Paik subjected line to the vulgarity of everyday life. *Zen for TV* (1958) is in part a parody, but Paik's joke was perhaps tinged with sadness and melancholy, too, about the lost ideals of abstraction.

With Pop Art exerting a significant effect in the United States in the 1960s, abstraction came under further attack. In *Estate* (1963) (fig. 2), in a deadpan if not sly fashion, Rauschenberg parenthetically indexed the color passages of Hans Hofmann on the margins of his montages of the explosive current events of the period. Andy Warhol created similar effects and, on occasion, juxtaposed a monochromatic field of color with a sea of images of a car crash (*Five Deaths, Seventeen Times in Black and White*, 1963), or the electric chair (*Silver Disaster*, 1963), or Elizabeth Taylor (*Liz*, 1965). Such contrasts

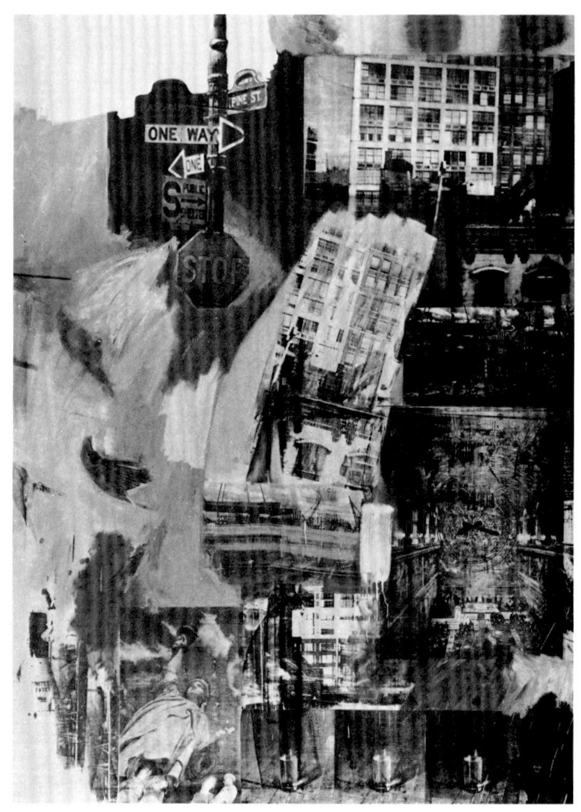

FIG. 2 Robert Rauschenberg
Estate, 1963. Oil and printer's ink on canvas, 96 × 70 inches. Philadelphia Museum of Art. Gift of the Friends of the Philadelphia Museum of Art

were more disconcerting than the critiques of the previous decade, for they seemed to suggest that by comparison abstract art appeared utterly inconsequential, even when poised next to someone as glamorously forgettable as Liz. Further mocking occurs in Tom Wesselman's *Still Life No. 20* (1962) wherein the abstract painting retains little of its dignity in a bathroom tableau. Richard Artschwager's intermittent series, *Windows* and *Mirrors*, of the late 1960s and after also proposed by their titles that monochrome compositions were absolutely not about a spiritual plane, as the pioneers of abstraction had proposed, but were rooted in and should be understood in the context of the world of appearances. Because Artschwager's objects in these series were usually formica, he demonstrated either that the moment had come for the blank, timeless canvas to be invested with a modern material, or, ironically, that the abstract icon carried as much meaning as a 1950s' kitchen table.

On the West Coast, Joe Goode (*Milk Bottle Painting,* 1961) and Ed Ruscha (*Ace*, 1962) put the monochrome format to other uses. As with Delaunay and Chagall, these artists juxtaposed elements of life with the bland and blank canvas. In 1967, John Baldessari attacked abstraction and the monochrome canvas with a joke about "articulation," a modernist, abstract convention of mark-making; he showed that words and language could provide articulation too. Just as the aforementioned paintings used the blank canvas as a backdrop or foil, Bruce Nauman, in *Ah Ha* (1975), repeated this technique while also proclaiming that the game was up, that abstraction's meaningfulness was, in fact, meaningless. An interesting aspect of the critiques posited by Ruscha, Baldessari, and Nauman concerned one of abstraction's most fundamental premises. The abstractionists, despising the ancient relationship of art to literature, had claimed a position of purity similar to that accorded to music. But these opponents returned language and its attributes in a quite literal fashion.

Roy Lichtenstein's *Non-objective* (1964) carried the critique of abstraction to a new level. Even if Lichtenstein in fact celebrated Mondrian here, he coarsened Mondrian's seriousness and attempts at a metaphysical subject matter by turning it into a comic-strip rendering. Deepening the force of his attack, Lichtenstein, perhaps for the first time, appropriated a well-known abstraction, thereby compromising and undercutting its originality. Little of substance seemed to differentiate Mondrian's signature composition and Lichtenstein's contemporaneous pictures of school-book covers; with both apparently mere patterns, abstraction had been stripped down to its decorative base. During the 1960s, Lichtenstein made a point of denuding abstract icons of their dignity. His *Brushstroke* series (1965) joked about the almighty gesture of the Abstract Expressionists who so epitomized the style at a high point in its history (fig. 3). Where is the heroism of the omnipotent creators, the unique personality implied by each artist's characteristic gesture? Lichtenstein's paintings possess as much of that quality as his comic-book couples exhibit the virtues of love. All idealism has been satirized and rendered sentimental by the artist, and abstraction's position as a carrier of the modern world and modernity itself has been powerfully compromised.

In Europe, too, the rush was on to give abstraction a thorough going-over. Sigmar Polke's *Modern Art* (1968) was a joke made from an insider's point of view, even though the stereotypical jeer—this is art?—was usually uttered by outsiders. Note that it is specifically an abstract image that stands for or is a sign of the modern, which is ridiculed. The attack becomes even more specific in Polke's send-up of Ellsworth Kelly, entitled *The Highest State: Painting Black Upper Right Corners* (1969). Here the American penchant for and celebration of formalist strategies has taken on a comical pretension and religiosity. Also in Germany, through the 1960s, Gerhard Richter was carefully deconstructing abstraction with seeming seriousness, but his color charts, which mimic commercial paint brochures, took the exalted approach to monochrome in vain. In France, Daniel Buren evolved a more complex approach by co-opting abstract strategies. Starting in the late 1960s, he utilized sheets of paper with striped patterns—certainly not compositions—to investigate and deconstruct interior and exterior locations. His signature gesture was the stripe, as was the case of a good abstractionist, but his stripe is a completely neutral—even neuter or, as Buren said, "banal"[1]—mark, applied in a quasi-sociological/political examination of public spaces. The result was abstraction, or perhaps Newman's "zip" again, being put to a better use, a function that had to do with the world and its actual characteristics. With Daniel Buren, abstraction's purity was endangered by external events and circumstances.

As the movement to critique abstraction has gathered even greater momentum in the last decade or so, it has developed a variety of bases. One thrust has to do with the apparent seamlessness of conventional abstract formulas and compositions—that these suggest a purity of vision and in some cases imply the possibility of a utopian world. Jasper Johns led the way in this area with works such as *Corpse and Mirror* (1976), which shows an apparently neutral abstract field uncomfortably conjoined with a nearly identical second that seems to have been marred: here it is as if abstraction's purity has been sullied. Johns's consciousness of himself in relation to the preceding generation of abstractionists is made clear by the title of one of his first major non-objective paintings, *Scent*

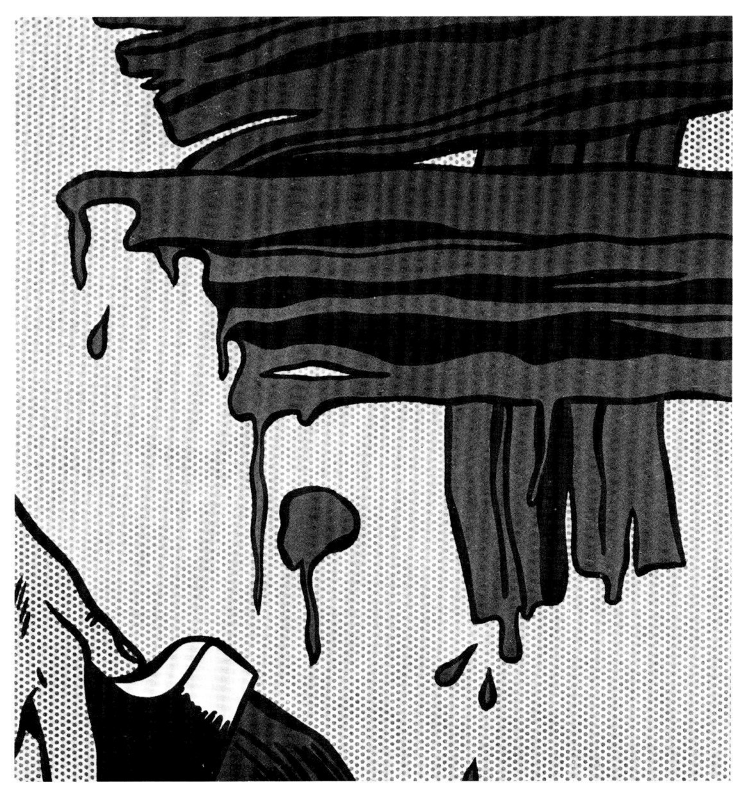

Fig. 3 Roy Lichtenstein
Brushstrokes, 1965. Oil and magna on canvas, 48 × 48 inches. ©Roy Lichtenstein

(1974), which echoes part of the title (*Lavender Mist*) of the last canvas (fig. 4) by Jackson Pollock, the great purveyor of continuous, infinite surfaces. Johns also created a sequel to a work by Newman, titling a painting *Voice 2* (1968–71).

Many younger painters, for instance Mary Heilmann and David Row, have furthered Johns's critique of the unsullied model of the world. These two artists are incorrigibly opposed to the appearance and implications of continuity or equilibrium. Instead, boundaries are crucial, either those that separate disparate areas or those that must be traversed if a hard-won but uneasy balance is to be achieved. Discontinuity is the hallmark of Row's paintings, with the perfection of the circle employed as a foil that is always being mooted. By contrast, a sense for the hybrid constantly pervades Heilmann's work, as well as the tendency to turn the lushness of earlier abstraction's colors into an all-out hothouse sensuality. Compared to the sense of a serene, neutral utopia that underlies abstraction, Heilmann and Row make world disorder the precondition for the new abstraction. Row describes the "abandonment of a Kantian ideal [and] the introduction of a fractured quality" so as to produce "a sense of the provisional and the legitimacy of subjective interpretation."[2] This kind of abstraction suggests that the preceding models were arid because of their seamlessness, and that they lacked a degree of the human drama that could give them life.

To further undo abstraction's complacent harmonies and unity, a certain air of deliberate, knowing awkwardness often pervades the work of younger artists. Jonathan Lasker, Mark Milloff, and David Reed, in particular, evince this quality, exaggeratedly calling attention to mark-making or articulation in the postmodern world. The characterization "dumb" comes to mind in contemplating such works, dumb like a fox, for intelligence and calculation abound in these paintings. Indeed, smart-ass abstraction is perhaps the better appellation. At first, Lasker's canvases seem heavy-

handed, almost slapstick demon-
strations of how an abstractionist
composes and balances the elements of form, line, and color.
Naming one series *Pre-fab View*
(1981), he satirizes the practices
and premises of high, which is to
say abstract, art. With his insou-
ciant candy-colors, he is a brat of
abstraction, having converted the
palette of the Abstract Expressionists to that of Disneyland.
But in the process, Lasker claims
a contemporary context for his
version of abstraction.

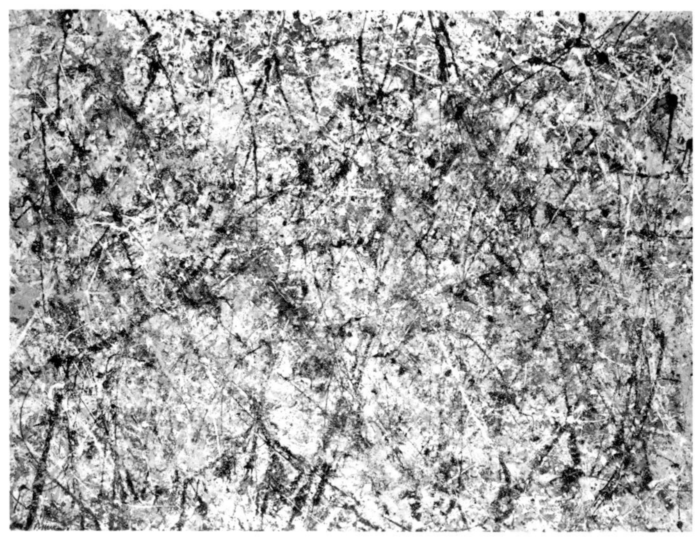

17

While also apparently awkward and impersonal, and involved with discon-
tinuous compositions and deconstructing the weighty brushstroke, Reed's work leads in
yet another direction. Always employing a format that echoes Pollock, Reed's critique
concerns abstraction's serenity. His color is lurid yet cool and artificial, like his gestures.
Just as the Baroque implanted heightened physicality and theatricality into the themes of
the Italian Renaissance, so Reed implodes earlier abstraction with a new energy.

Milloff, too, offers a very self-conscious, postmodern approach to mark-
making. Literally deconstructed, his art often consists of a richly painted canvas together with gobs of paint that have apparently fallen to the floor. The result is disconcerting,
for suddenly abstraction's dignity and unity are undone. One work, titled *Fallen Target II*

(1993), implies that Milloff's activity furthers the efforts of Johns to dismantle abstraction.

Notwithstanding their almost irreverent outlook and sometime tendency to abstraction, Heilmann, Lasker, Milloff, Reed, and Row all practice a pure, non-referential form of abstraction. They seek to recast the genres of abstraction without changing its primary non-objective appearance. By contrast, Ross Bleckner, Peter Halley, and Andres Serrano seek ways to infuse an explicit sense of the actual world, and even a degree of *Weltschmerz*, into this style, as if the preceding era of abstraction needed juice of some kind. Their approach is based on impersonating abstract styles, with the viewer gradually discovering that a serious and purposeful hoax has been perpetrated.

Serrano is a photographer who is hardly thought of in the context of abstraction. However, in each series of works, he almost systematically investigates various practices and expectations of art. So as to undo the pretense of purity, as well as the emphasis on an aesthetic emotion imparted solely by formal relationships, Serrano tells the viewer (by the titles of one group of apparently abstract images) that his photographed white is milk and that the red is blood. Even the perfect, ethereal circle has been filled with blood. Showing that the abstractionists' symbolism of color and form has disembowelled itself, he quite literally fleshes out this style. As with Johns and Nauman, Serrano works in the diptych format but reinvests it with the kinds of subject matter found in historical, religious diptychs. (Recall the milk of the Madonna that fed Jesus or Christ's blood.) Serrano has replaced the spirituality of Barnett Newman's and Brice Marden's diptychs with a transcendence founded on earthly substances.

Best known for paintings that impersonate 1960s' style abstractions composed of parallel lines or patterns of polka dots, Bleckner lulls the viewer into imagining his intentions are those of Op Art. Then the observer begins to realize that something lies beneath the patterns, that through the diaphanous abstract curtain is a referential realm often concerned with the scourge of AIDS. Bleckner's critique in part disputes earlier abstractionists' claim to communicate subliminally and even mystically through composition. Instead, he proposes a more explicit approach, along with a substantive subject matter. Compared to the exquisite and lofty subtlety of his predecessors, Bleckner's measured directness accords with the nature of contemporary life.

Halley, too, demonstrates a new type of synthesis between abstract form and worldly content, his goal being to suggest that his geometrical patterns are synonymous with prison and battery-cell construction. He writes: "The paintings are a critique of idealist modernism. In the 'color' field is placed a jail. The misty space of Rothko is walled up. The 'stucco' texture is a reminiscence of motel ceilings. The Day-Glo paint is a signifier of 'low-budget mysticism.' It is the afterglow of radiation."[3]

For Halley, abstract geometry should not be self-referential but possess "social meaning."[4] Furthermore, the cheeriness of his colors, which recall Pop Art rather than Abstract Expressionism, infuses the current cultural context, especially advertising, into his art. When Halley calls his work "diagrammatic,"[5] he again distinguishes himself from earlier abstract artists whose interest was to impart meaning as if by osmosis. He wishes to spell things out deliberately and clearly. In his most recent works, Halley creates a diagram of chaos occurring amongst his signature structures.

As might be expected, matters of gender and race have become aspects of the tendency to critique abstraction. Rachel Lachowicz creates wonderfully witty parodies of abstraction's masculine heroes. A work entitled *Sarah* (1991) (fig. 5) is Richard Serra's *One Ton Prop (House of Cards)* (1969) in drag, for it, along with *Homage to Carl Andre* (1991), has been recast from steel into lipstick. Using eyeliner, too, she reconstitutes an anonymous, painted male geometric composition. Rosemarie Trockel introduces stereotypically female practices, knitting and weaving, so as to reinterpret abstract media and

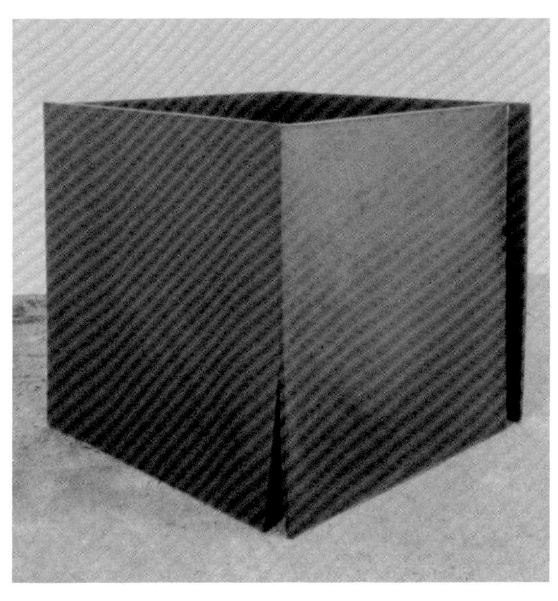

20

supports and, incidentally, to recall that one of the first abstractionists, Sophie Täuber-Arp, wove her compositions. Lachowicz and Trockel, in effect, feminize abstraction, replacing its impervious "male" materials with richly female scents and textures. This approach gives abstraction the possibility of being gender specific to women, too. Annette Lemieux skillfully adds race to the roll-call of concerns absent in abstraction, for in *Available Portrait Colors* (1990) (not included in this exhibition) and *Anonymity* (1992) she reproduces paint-sample catalogues that claim to show skin tones but which, nevertheless, neglect the full range of possibilities. With these critiques, Lachowicz, Trockel, and Lemieux bring a socially-conscious attitude to abstraction.

Abstraction's long-developed seriousness and pretensions are, in the present context, regularly parodied and even cheapened. For instance, Jonathan Borofsky juxtaposes life and the apparently mystical object—but the mystical object's demand for silent, adoring contemplation is undone by the mindless chatter of the mechanical observer. The abstract art object is a much diminished entity here, as it is in Lemieux's *Black Mass* (1991). One wonders if the Chinese marchers carrying placards are campaigning for or protesting the void that was represented by Malevich's black square paintings. At any rate, the precious "pure feelings" that so preoccupied the Russian painter are no longer safely enshrined in the museum setting but have simply become well-designed patterns taken to the streets. Lemieux's act is provocatively aggressive in a Marxist sense, for Malevich, unlike many of his Russian contemporaries, never quite believed in the new revolutionary government. Lemieux's work subjects his prized individuality to the conditions of daily life.

Like Lemieux, Allan McCollum seems to have appropriated one of the most significant of abstraction's icons, for his paintings are too similar to Malevich's not to have been inspired by them. If one recalls Malevich's ardent interest in the expressive content of each of his canvases, then McCollum has not only cheapened the Russian's ambitions but, by emphasizing commodification and a seemingly random, even chaotic, multiplication of images, has relegated Malevich's unique creations to the junkheap of cheap, touristic trinkets. Calling these multiples "plaster surrogates" or "pseudo-artifacts,"[6] McCollum restores a common nothing to the revered Nothing, much as Artschwager did.

In the hands of Sherrie Levine, too, the originality of gesture and the preserve of unique personality—hallmarks of the aesthetics of abstraction and art in general—are diminished. She approaches the issue by using the appropriationist technique of the simulacrum, discussed so eloquently by Jean Baudrillard. She carefully copies the original of an historic work, thus making a signboard of the abstract vision. In doing so, Levine takes a powerful step toward undermining both the signifier and the signified. With the icon transmuted for use in a postmodern iconography, the original work of art loses its authority, preciousness, mysticism, value, and prestige. Levine's cunning practice turns intended sacred objects into sanctimonious relics.

Abstraction's longevity through the century, it could be argued, is due to the unceasingly Romantic nature of art and the social and philosophical underpinnings of the period. But current investigations of this style are symptomatic of an erosion of those earlier attitudes in favor of a more analytical, pragmatic, ironic, or even cynical point of view. For instance, underlying virtually all critiques of abstraction is an attack on its semblance of liberation, so often declared by the great practitioners. Whereas Barnett Newman imagined that his artistic strategy demonstrated unparalleled freedom and even anarchy, recent artists hold that his notion is an illusion in the real world, where all individuals are influenced and their actions compromised by the circumstances of life. As a corollary, if the modern outlook saw social commitment in utopian terms, the current, postmodern approach demands greater directness and accountability. It is noteworthy, however, that the individuals discussed here have not so much chosen to do away with their predecessors' imagery as to reinterpret and reform it. This reliance on abstraction reveals not only a certain lingering nostalgia, but shows that its visual qualities continue to have potential even in the postmodern era. Nevertheless, by these artists' actions, the icons of abstraction are left for the viewer in a state similar to the Mona Lisa after Marcel Duchamp drew her with a moustache.

Notes

1   Cited in Jerome Sans, "Daniel Buren," *Forum Internation*, 9 (September 1991), p. 36.

2   David Row, "A Conversation with Demetrio Paparoni," *Tema Celeste*, 34 (January–March 1992), p. 95.

3   Peter Halley, "Notes on the Paintings," in *Peter Halley, Collected Writings 1981–87* (Venice, CA: Lapis Press, 1991), p. 23.

4   Cited in Michael Schwartz, "Peter Halley," *Galleries Magazine*, 46 (December 1991/January 1992), p. 79.

5   Cited in Jeanne Siegel, "The Artist/Critic of the Eighties, Part One: Peter Halley and Stephen Westfall," *Arts*, 60:1 (September 1985), p. 73.

6   Cited in Craig Owens, "Allan McCollum: Repetition & Difference," *Art in America* (September 1983), p. 130.

Plates

Richard Artschwager   *Mirror, 1988. Formica and enamel on wood, $30\frac{3}{8} \times 24\frac{3}{8} \times 3\frac{7}{8}$ inches*

John Baldessari   *A Two-Dimensional Surface Without Any Articulation is a Dead Experience*, 1967. Acrylic on canvas, $57\,^3/_8 \times 67\,^1/_2$ inches

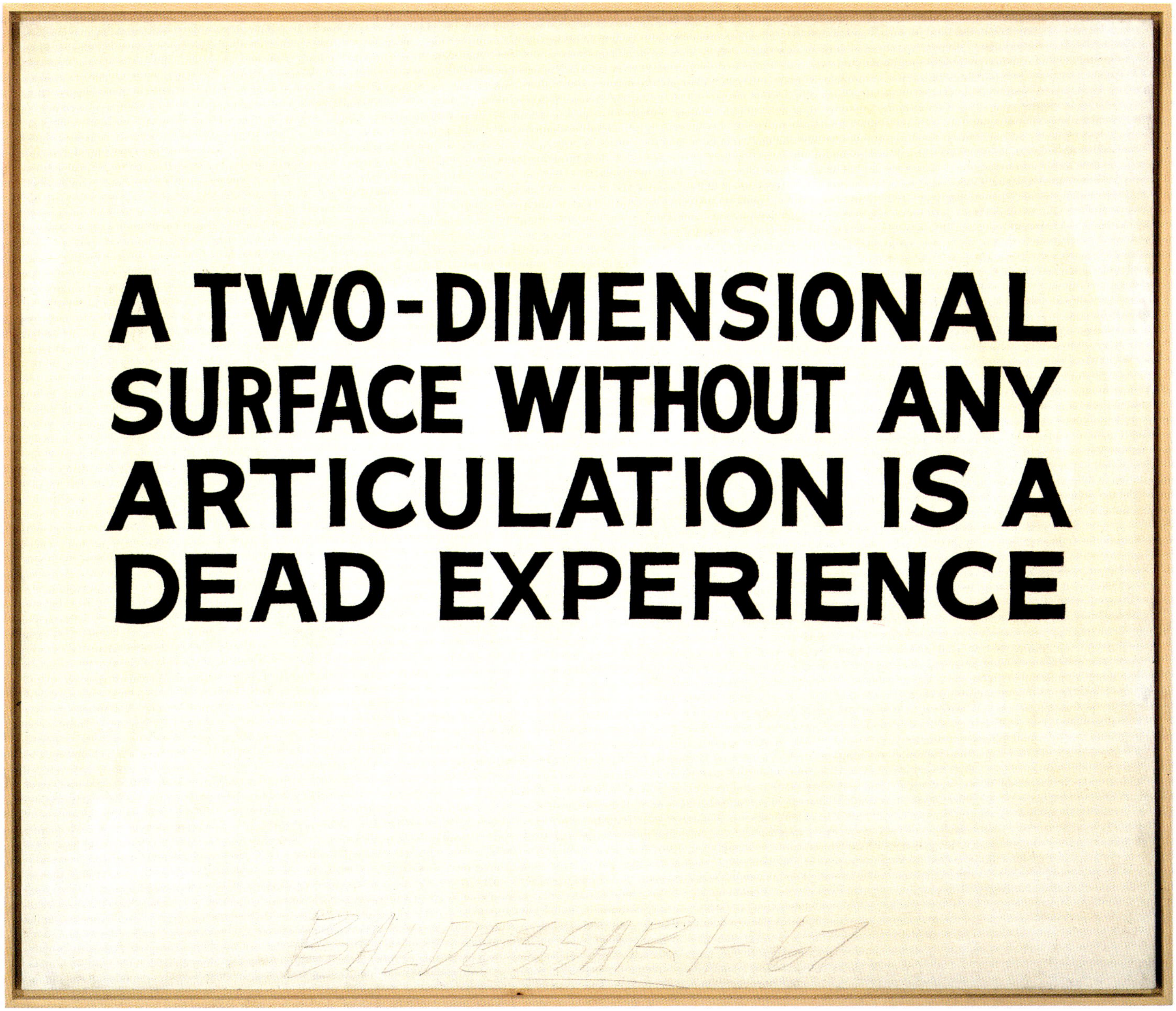

A TWO-DIMENSIONAL
SURFACE WITHOUT ANY
ARTICULATION IS A
DEAD EXPERIENCE

BALDESSARI-67

Ross Bleckner *Gold Count No Count*, 1991. Oil on canvas, 96 × 72 inches

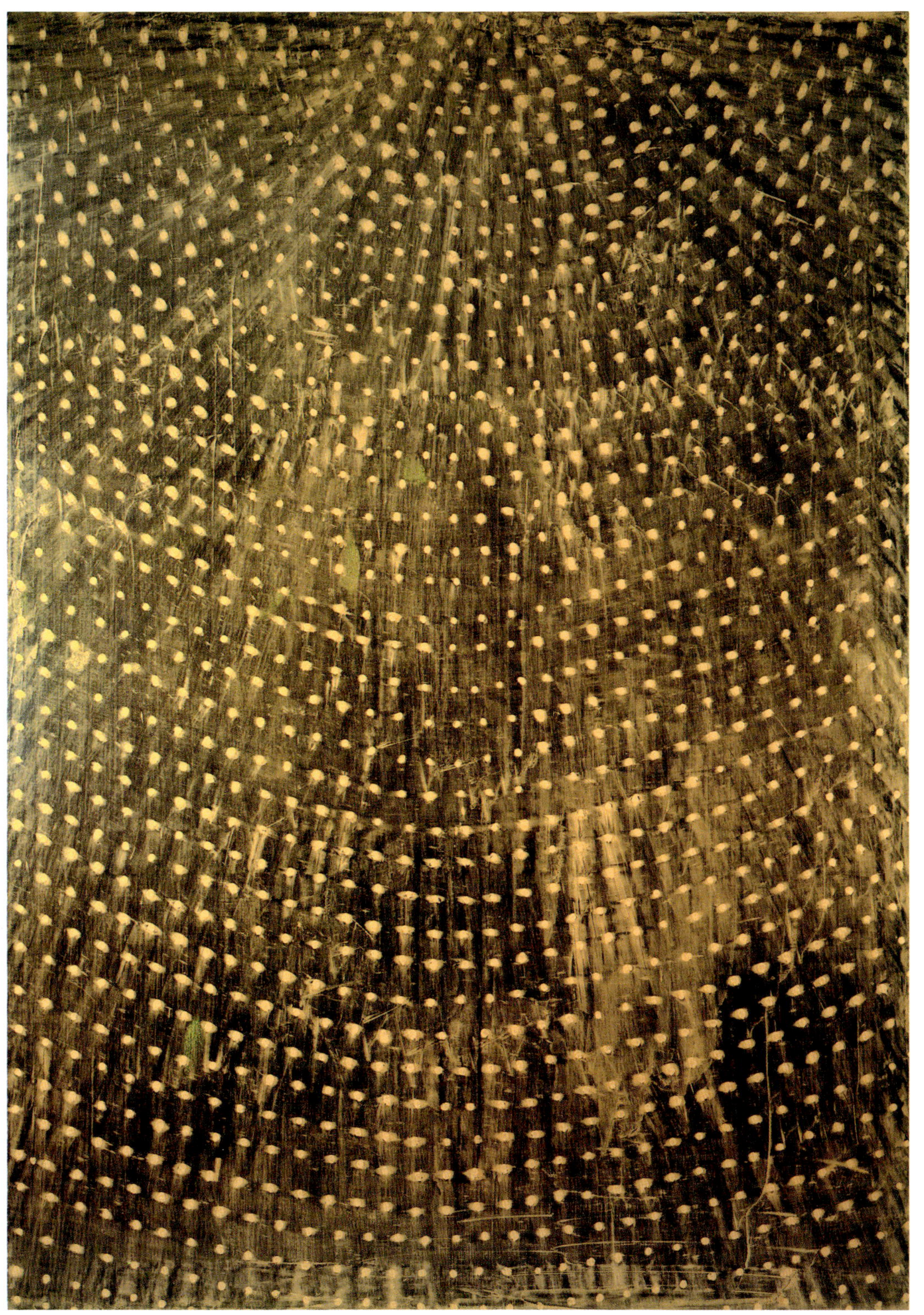

Jonathan Borofsky   *Untitled at 2,835,666* with *Chattering Man*, 1983. *Untitled at 2,835,666*: Ink and oil on paper, 80 × 101 inches

Chattering Man: Mixed media, 80 × 23 × 13 inches

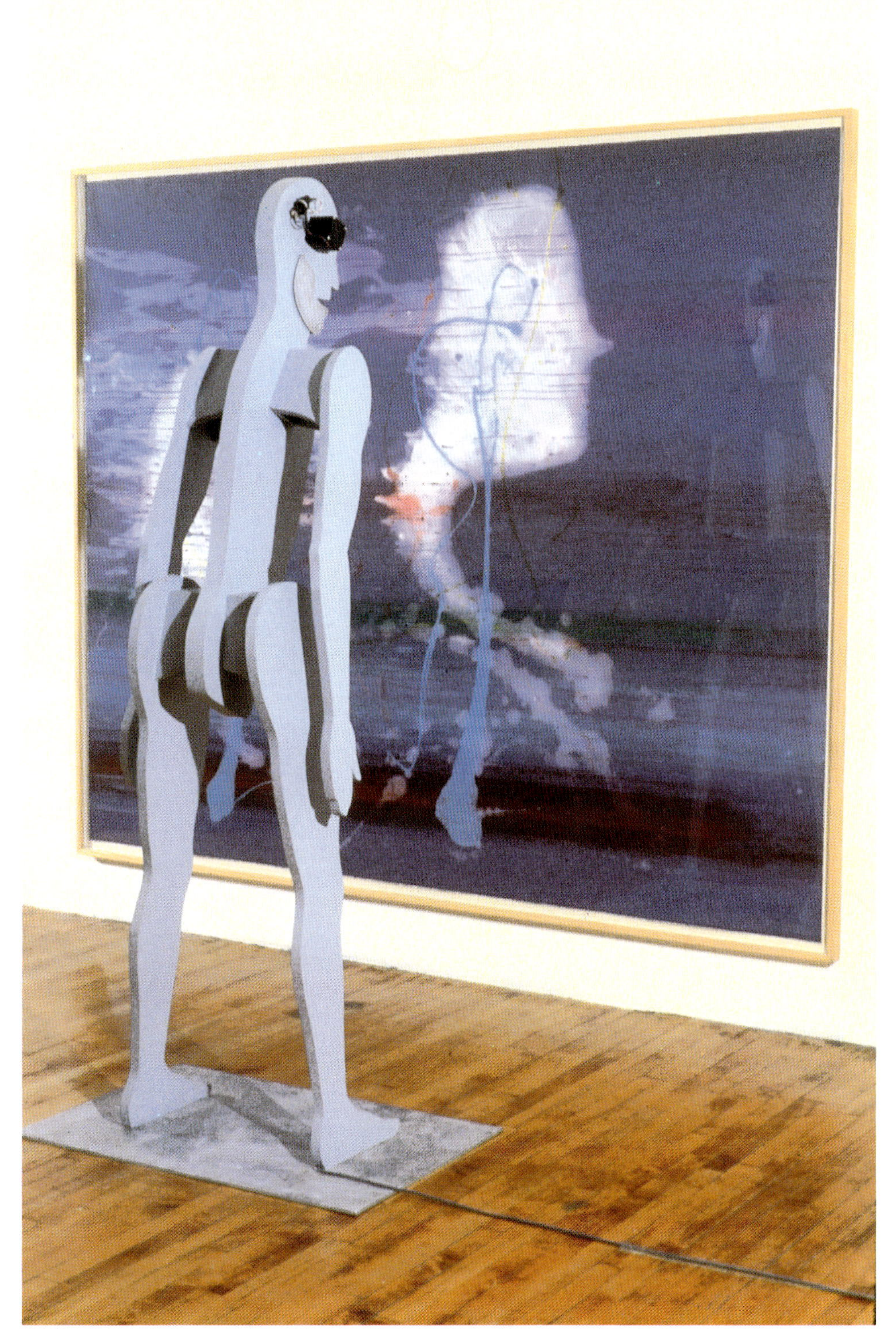

D a n i e l   B u r e n   *Framed/Exploded/Defaced*, 1979. Color aquatint etchings, 25 fragments, $8 \times 8 \times \frac{1}{2}$ inches each, overall dimensions variable

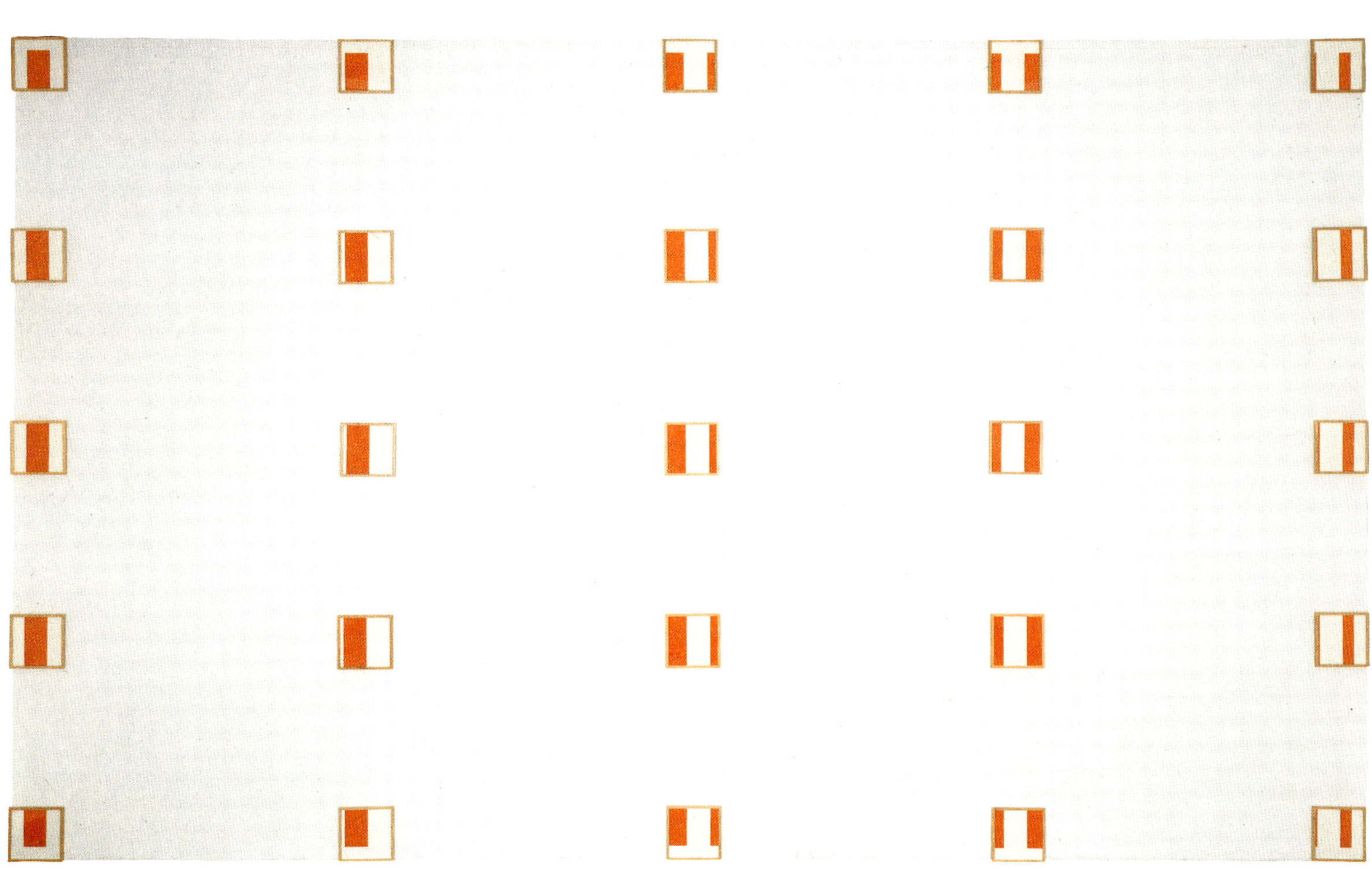

Peter Halley   *303*, 1991. Day-Glo acrylic, acrylic, and Roll·A·Tex on canvas, 88 ½ × 91 ½ inches

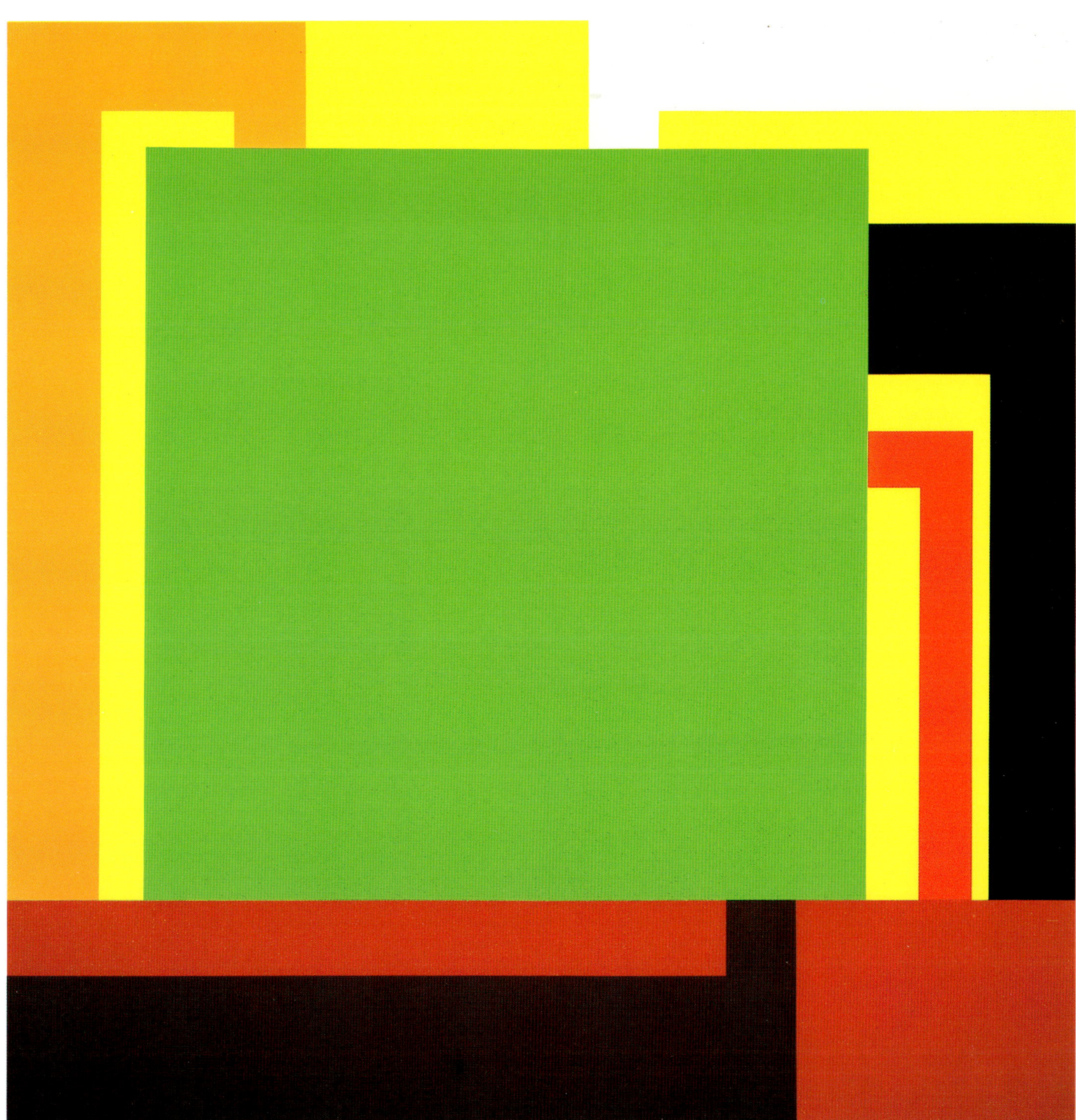

Mary Heilmann   *Peter Young*, 1990. Oil on canvas, 54 × 54 inches

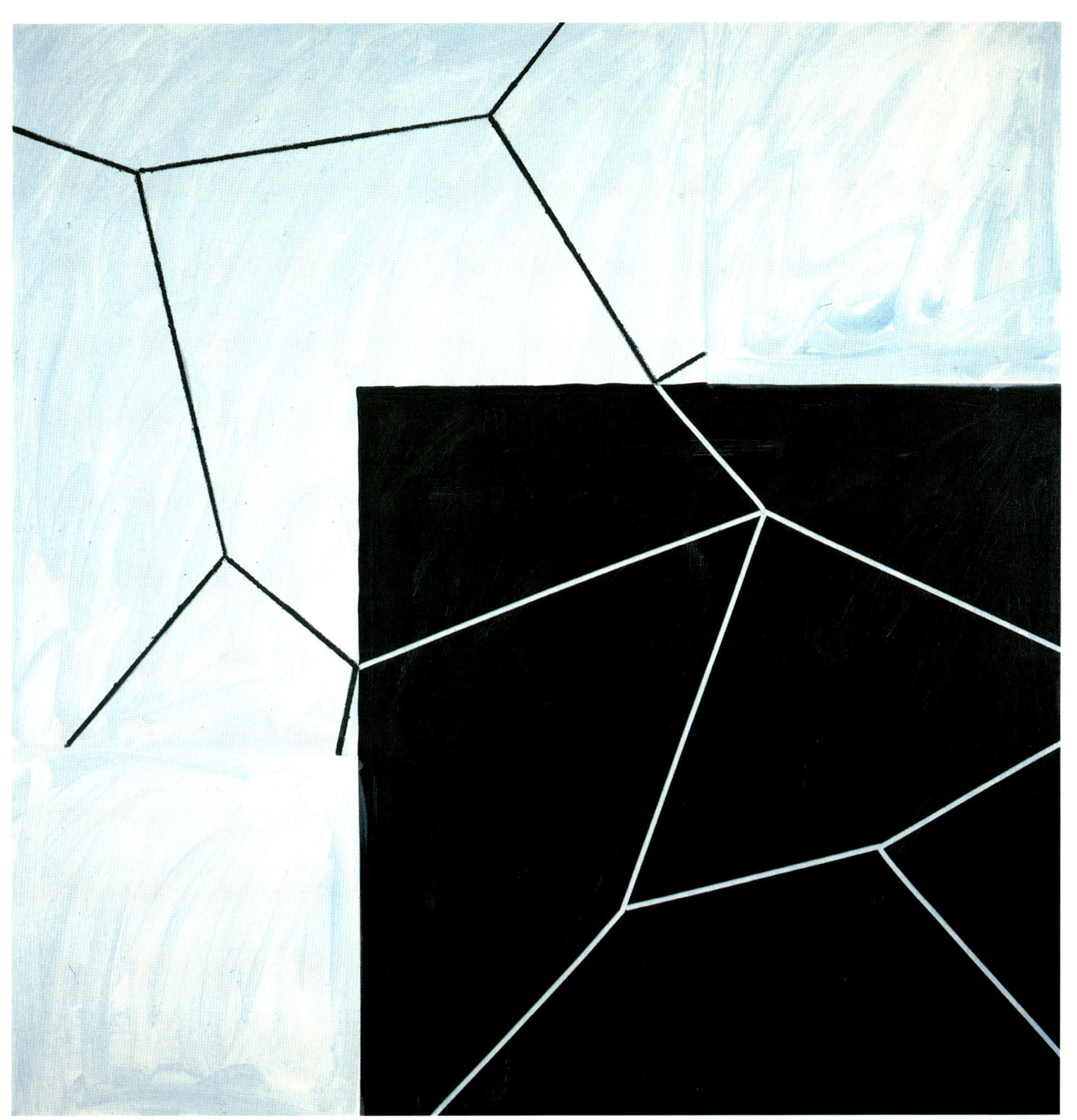

J a s p e r   J o h n s   *Corpse and Mirror*, 1976. Lithograph, 30 ¾ × 39 ⅝ inches. ©1995 Jasper Johns / VAGA, New York

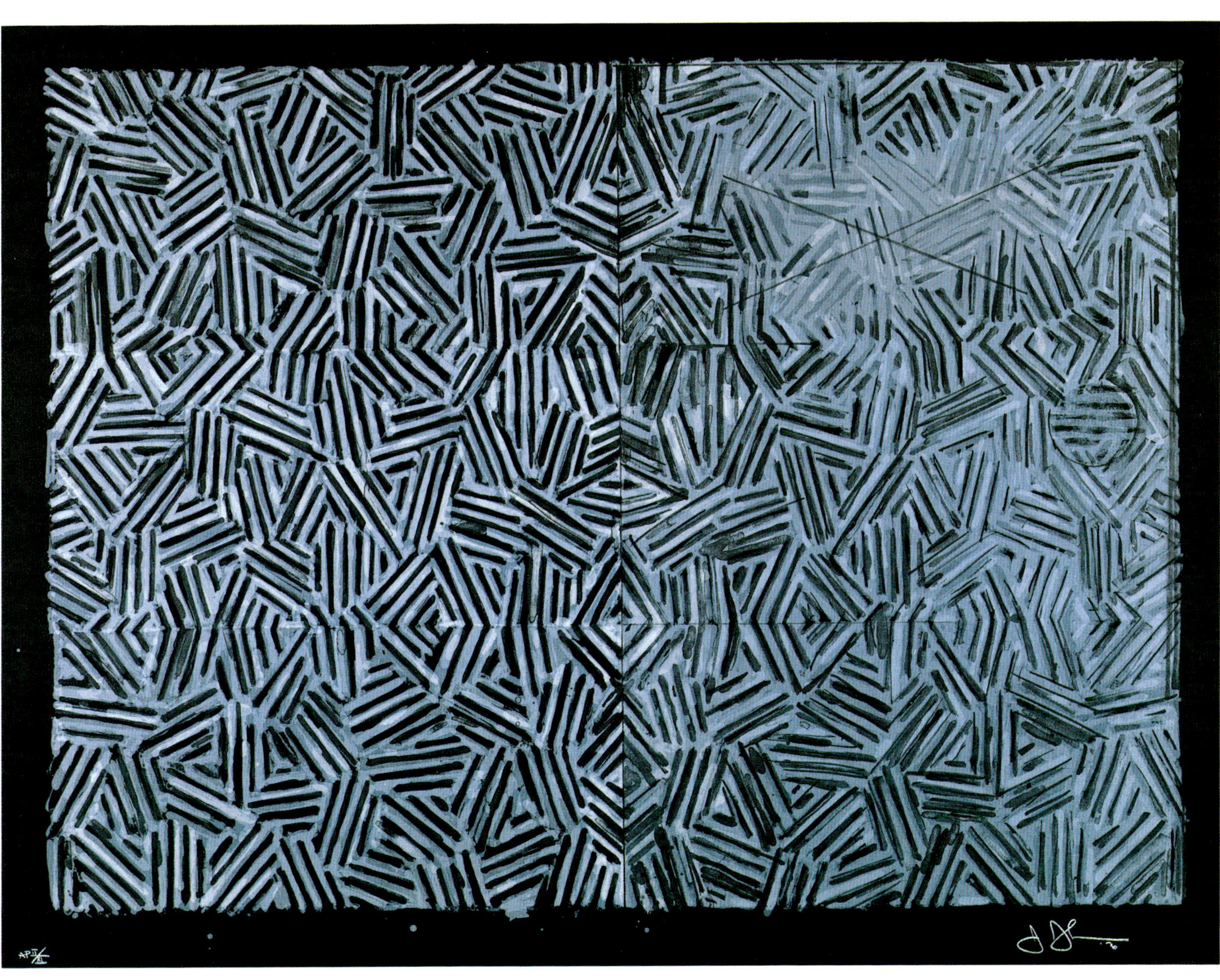

R a c h e l   L a c h o w i c z   *Homage to Carl Andre*, 1991/1994. Lipstick and wax, $\frac{3}{8} \times 72 \times 72$ inches

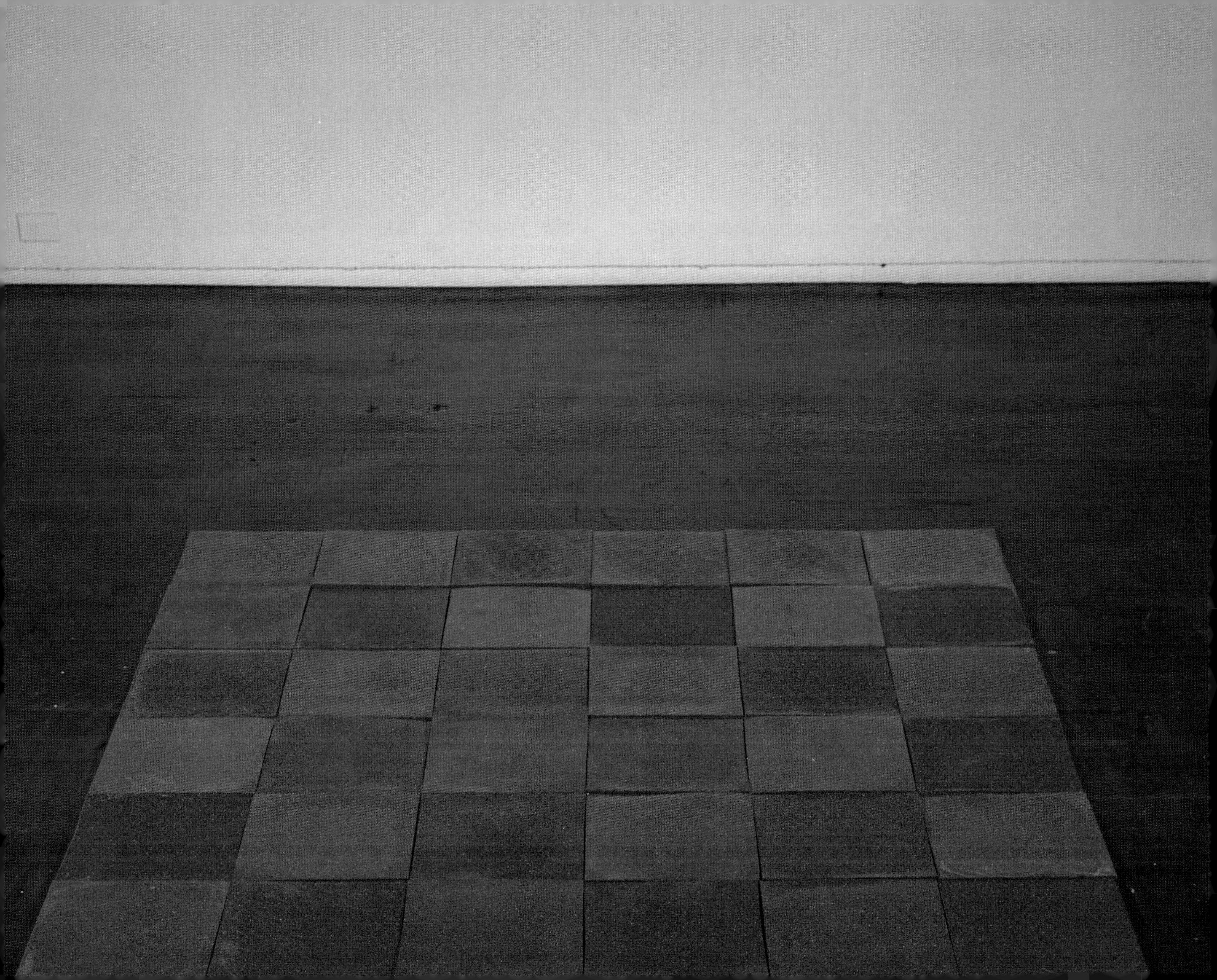

Jonathan Lasker *The Happiness of Cannibals*, 1991. Oil on linen, 52 ½ × 63 inches

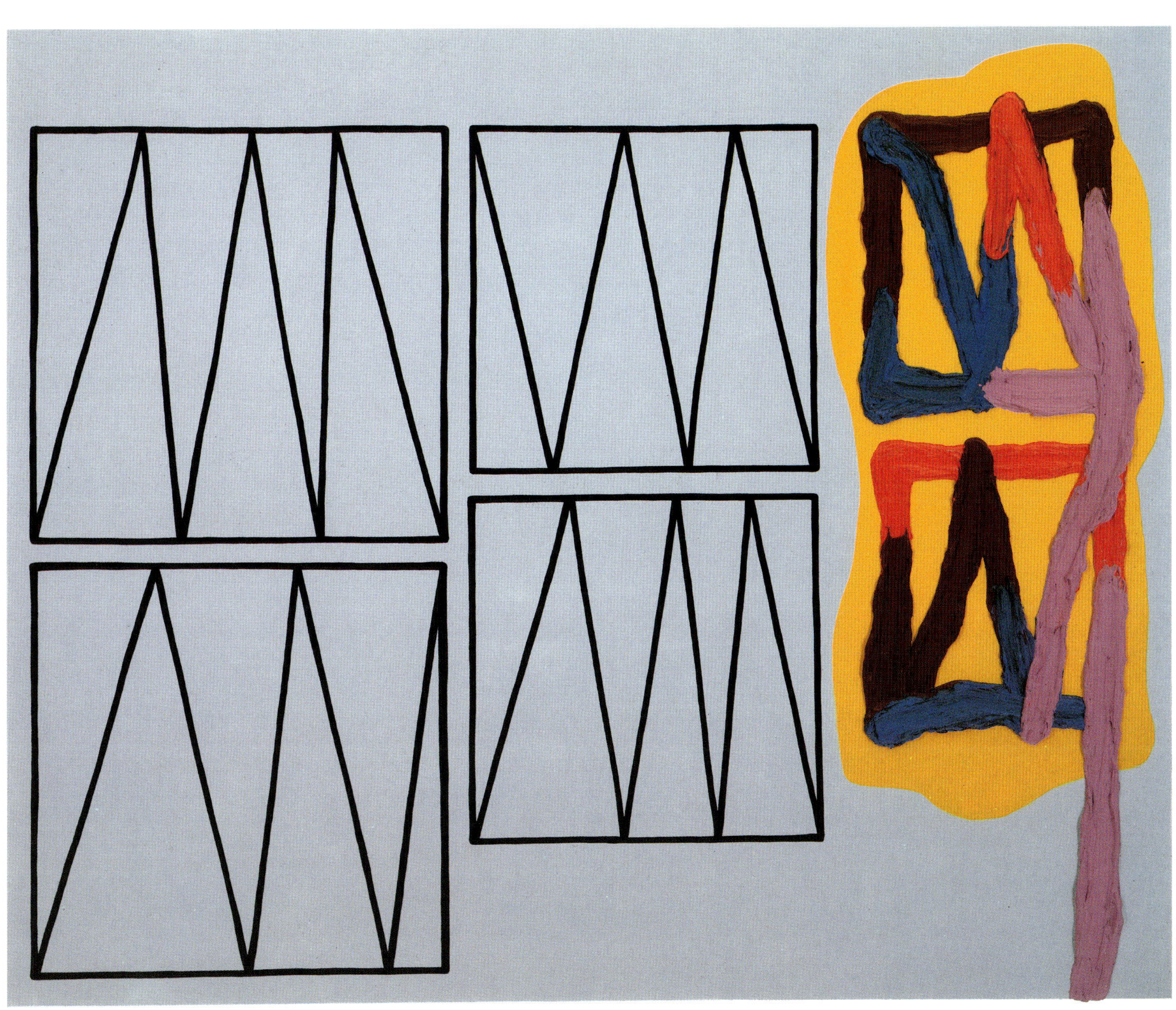

A n n e t t e   L e m i e u x   *Anonymity*, 1992. Oil and gesso on canvas, 72 × 66 inches

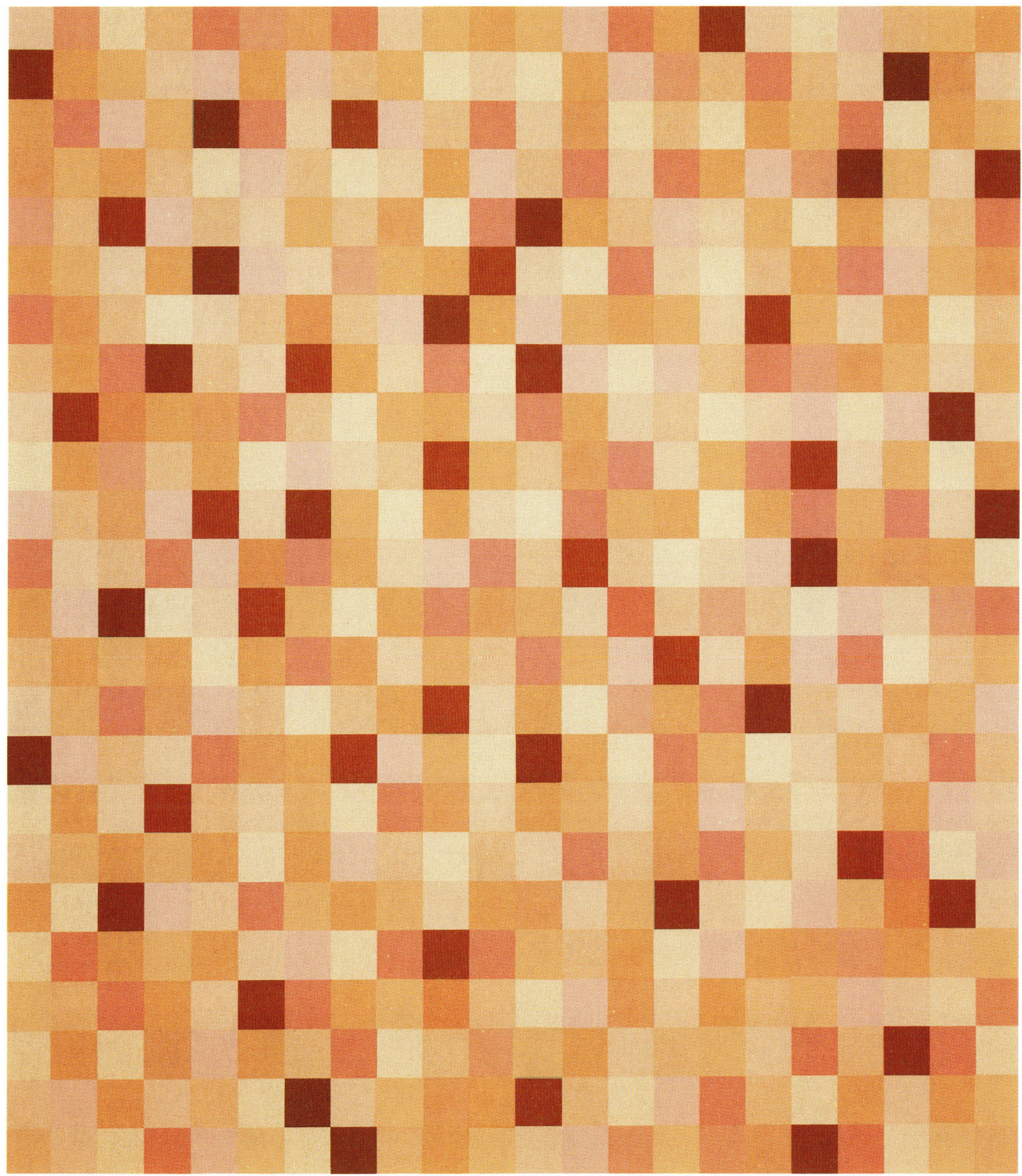

S h e r r i e   L e v i n e   *Medium Check: 12,* 1985. Casein and wax on mahogany, 24 × 20 inches

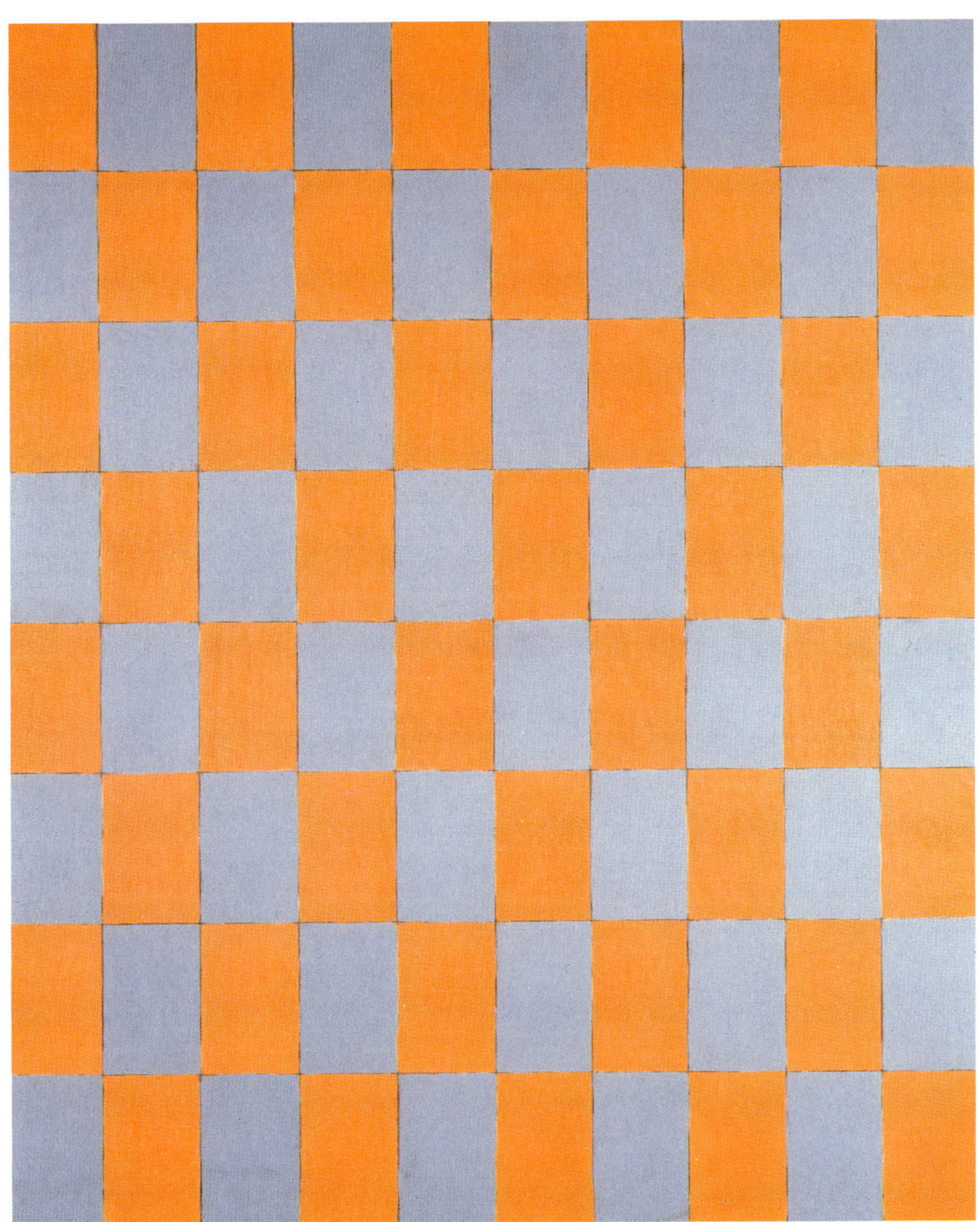

A l l a n   M c C o l l u m   *10 Plaster Surrogates*, 1982/92. Enamel on solid cast Hydrocal, 10 parts, dimensions variable, 24 × 168 inches overall

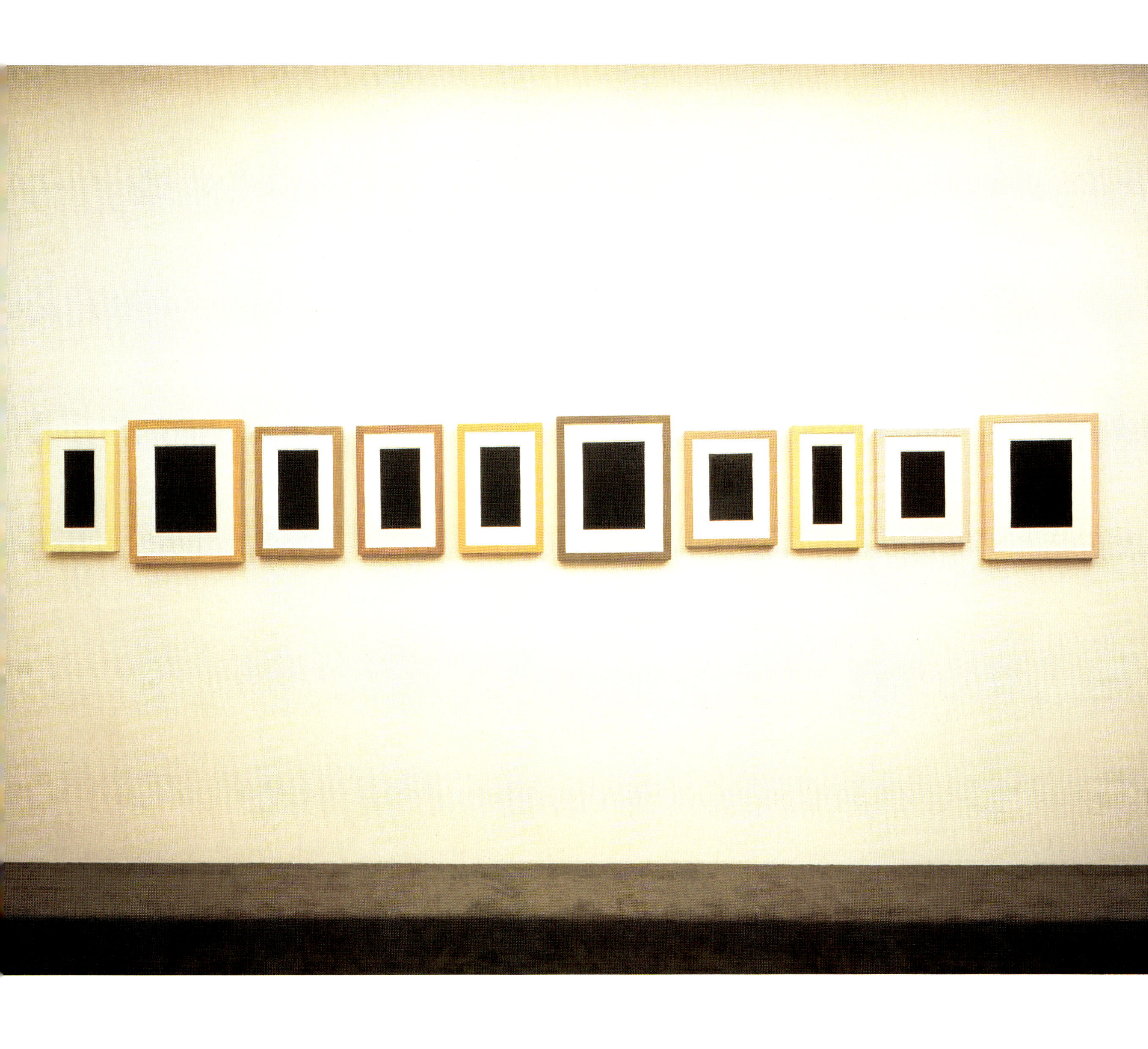

Mark   Milloff   *Untitled (Bars)*, 1993. Oil on canvas, 48 × 30 inches

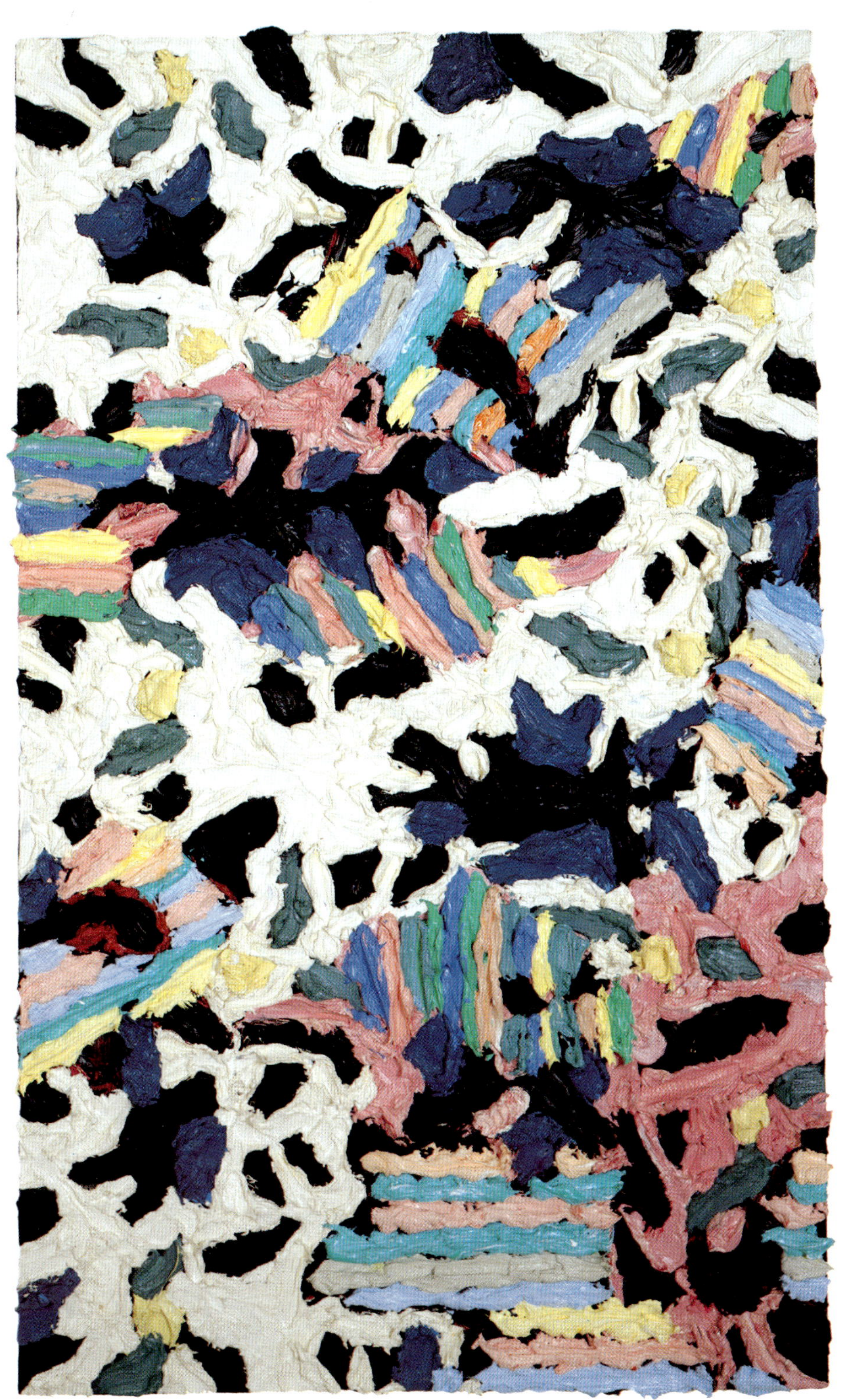

B r u c e   N a u m a n *Ah Ha*, 1975. One-color screenprint, 29 $\frac{1}{8}$ × 41 $\frac{1}{8}$ inches

AH

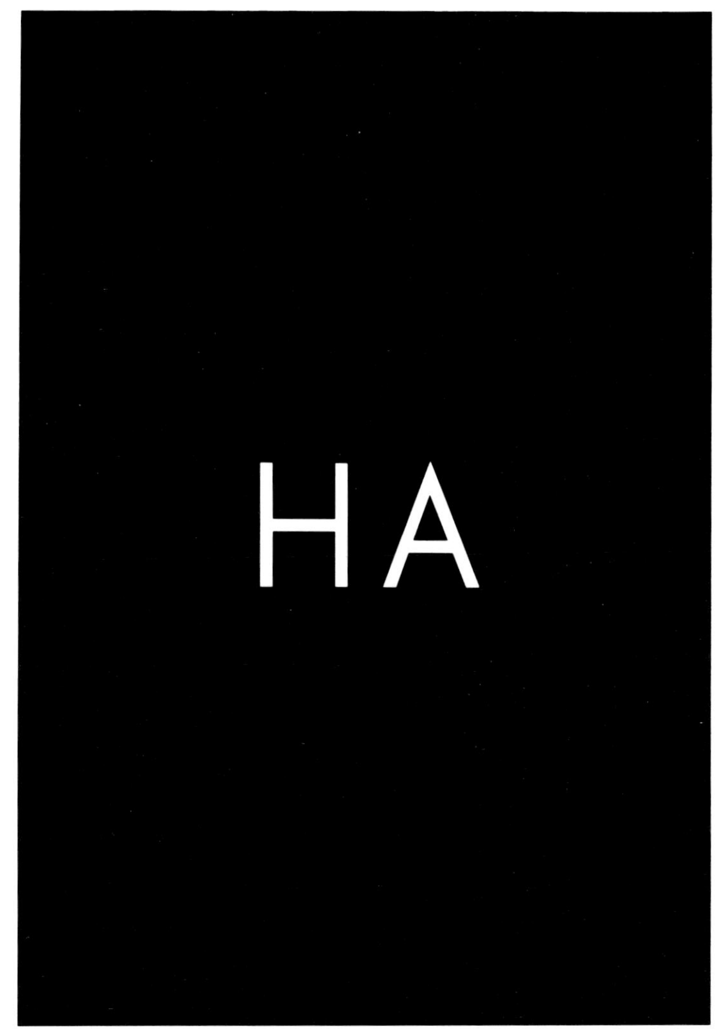

N a m   J u n e   P a i k   *Zen for TV*, 1975–94. Video sculpture, 16 × 12 ¹⁄₂ × 16 inches

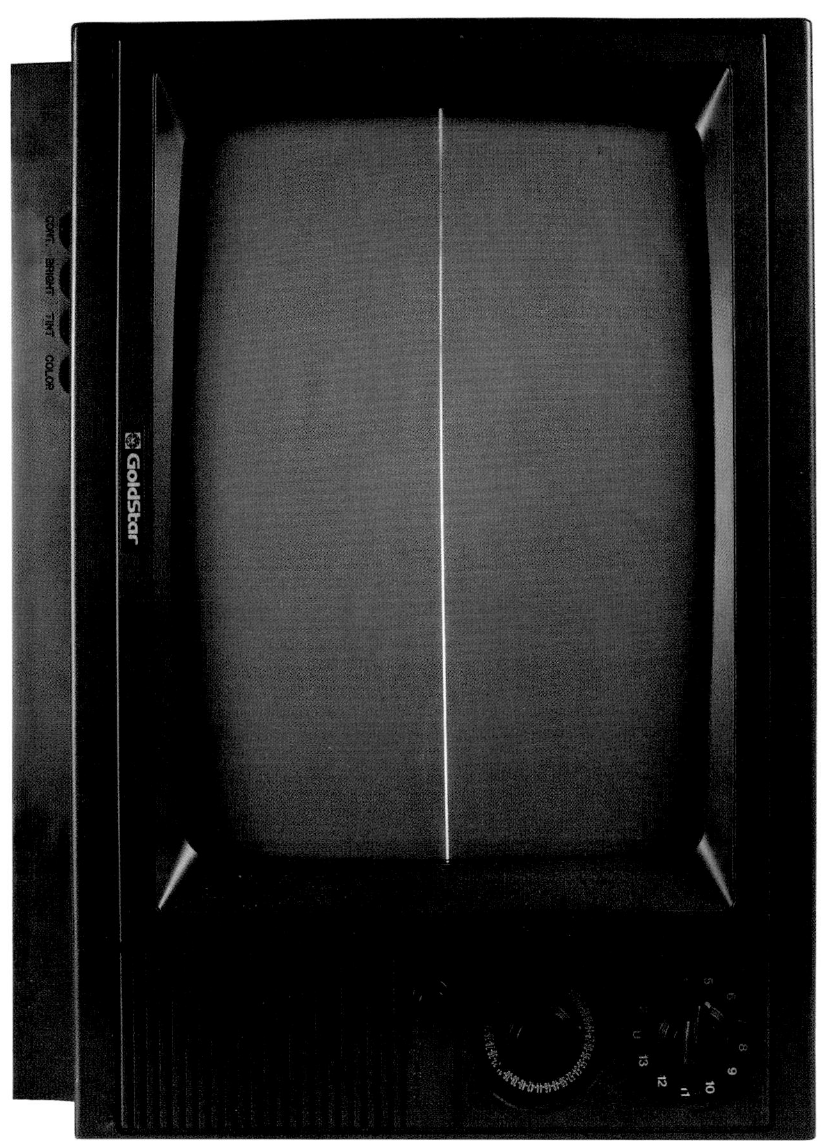

GoldStar
CONT.
BRIGHT
TINT
COLOR

D a v i d   R e e d   *No. 269, 1989. Oil and alkyd on linen, 27 × 103 inches*

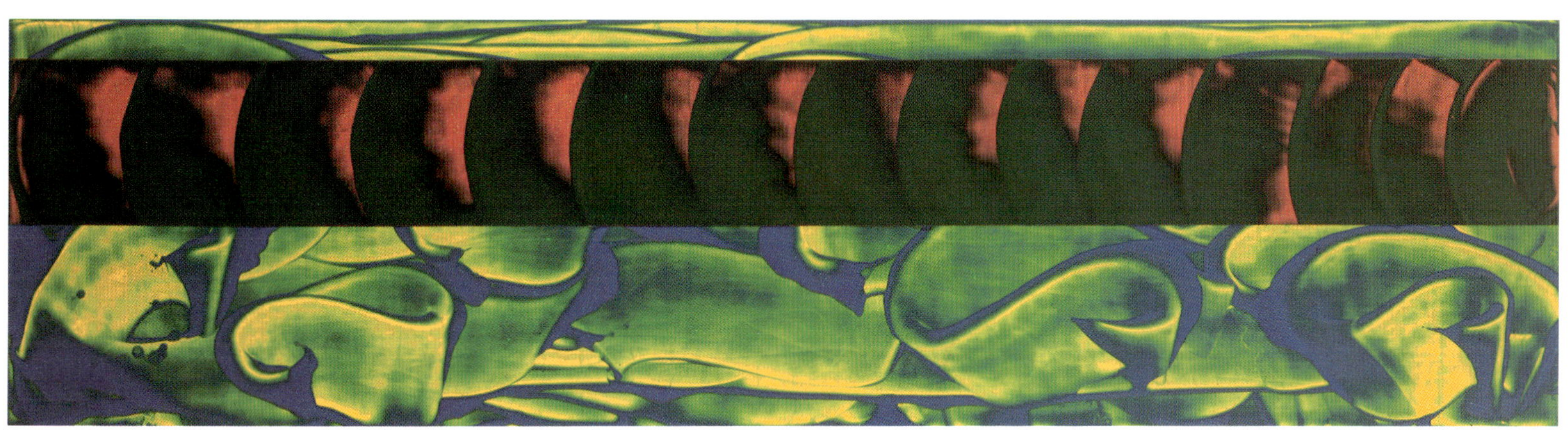

D a v i d   R o w   *Split Infinitive*, 1990. Oil and wax on canvas, 86 × 116 inches

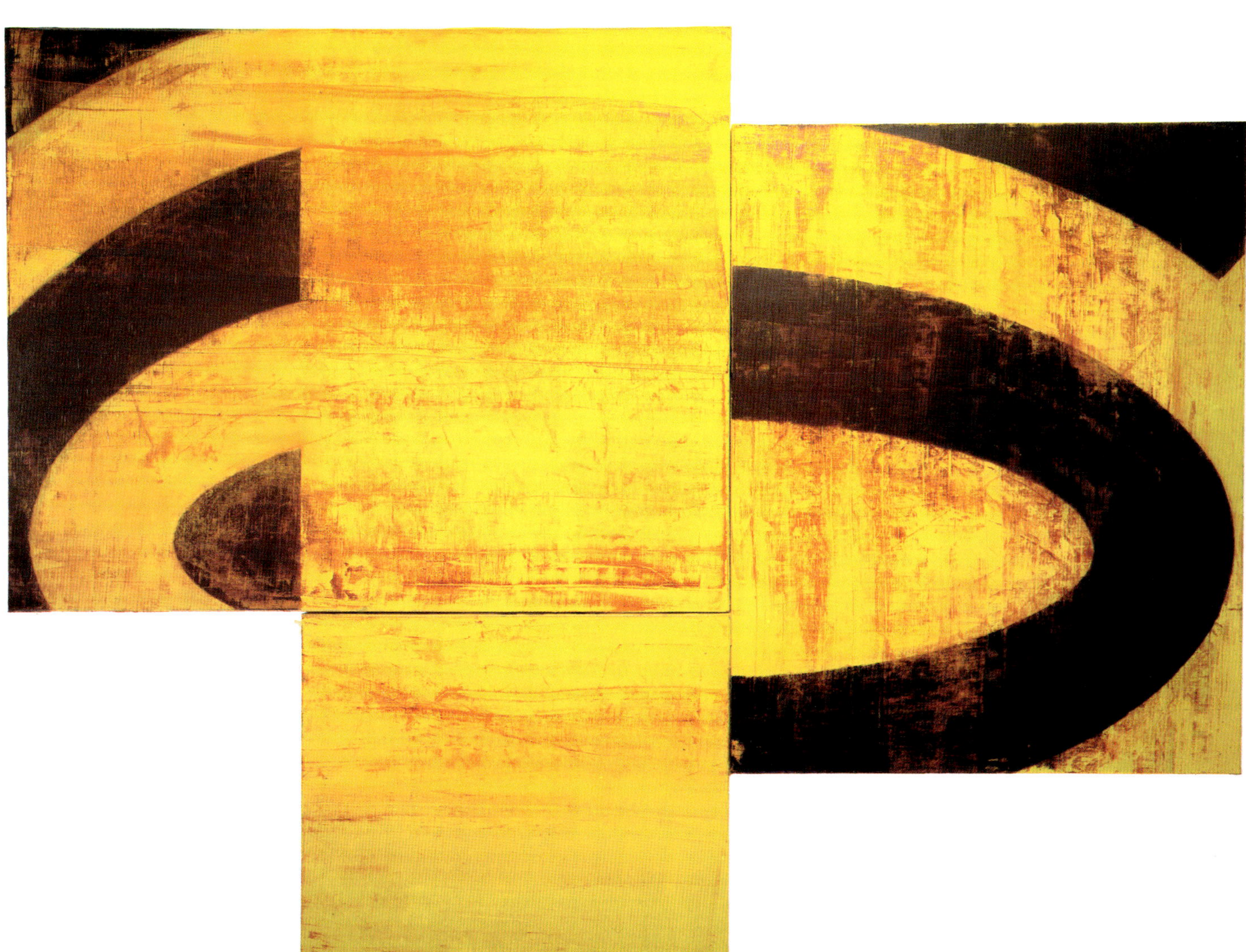

A n d r e s   S e r r a n o   *Circle of Blood*, 1987. Cibachrome, 40 × 60 inches

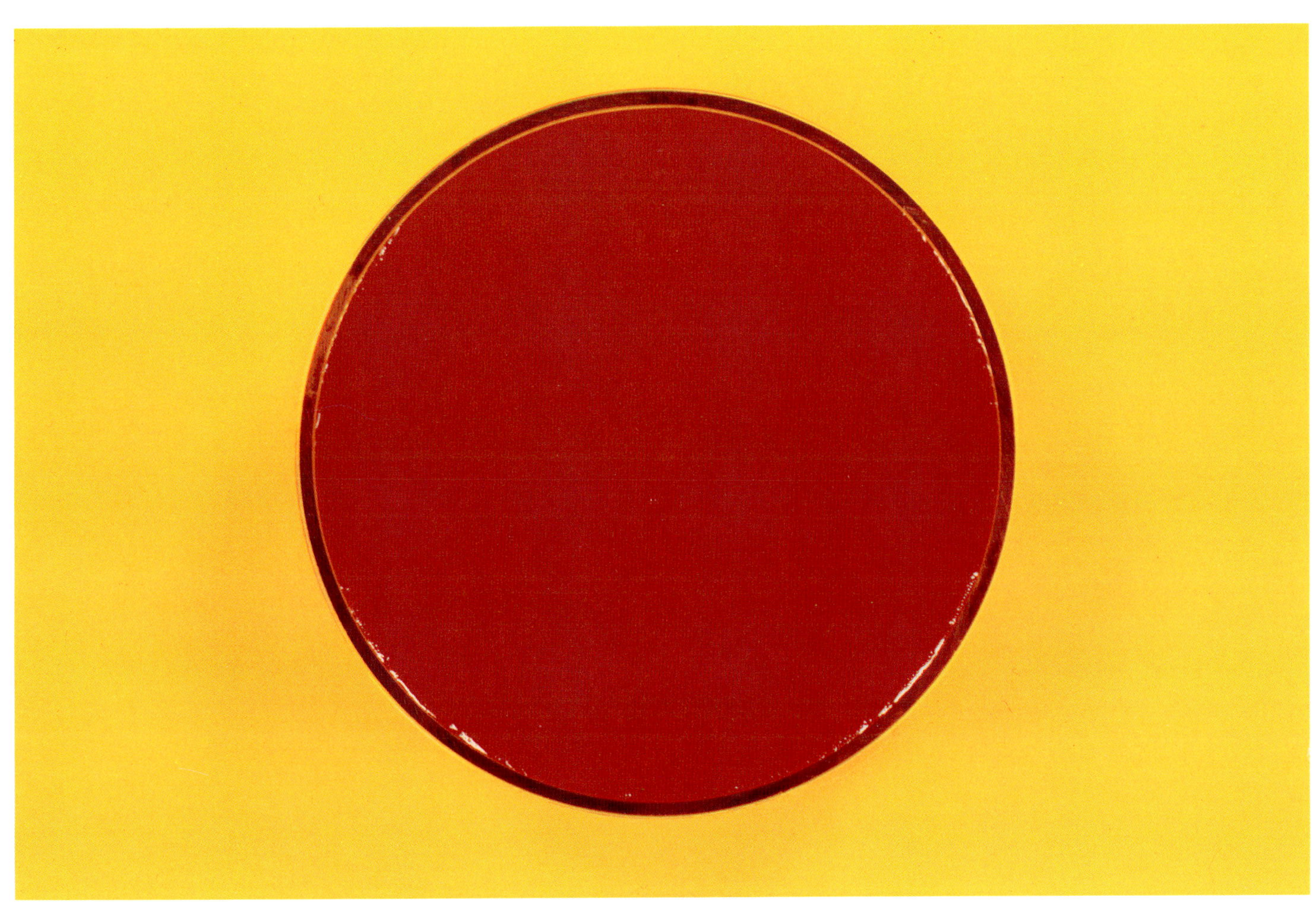

R o s e m a r i e   T r o c k e l   *Untitled*, 1987. Knitted wool, 59 ⅝ × 35 ¾ inches

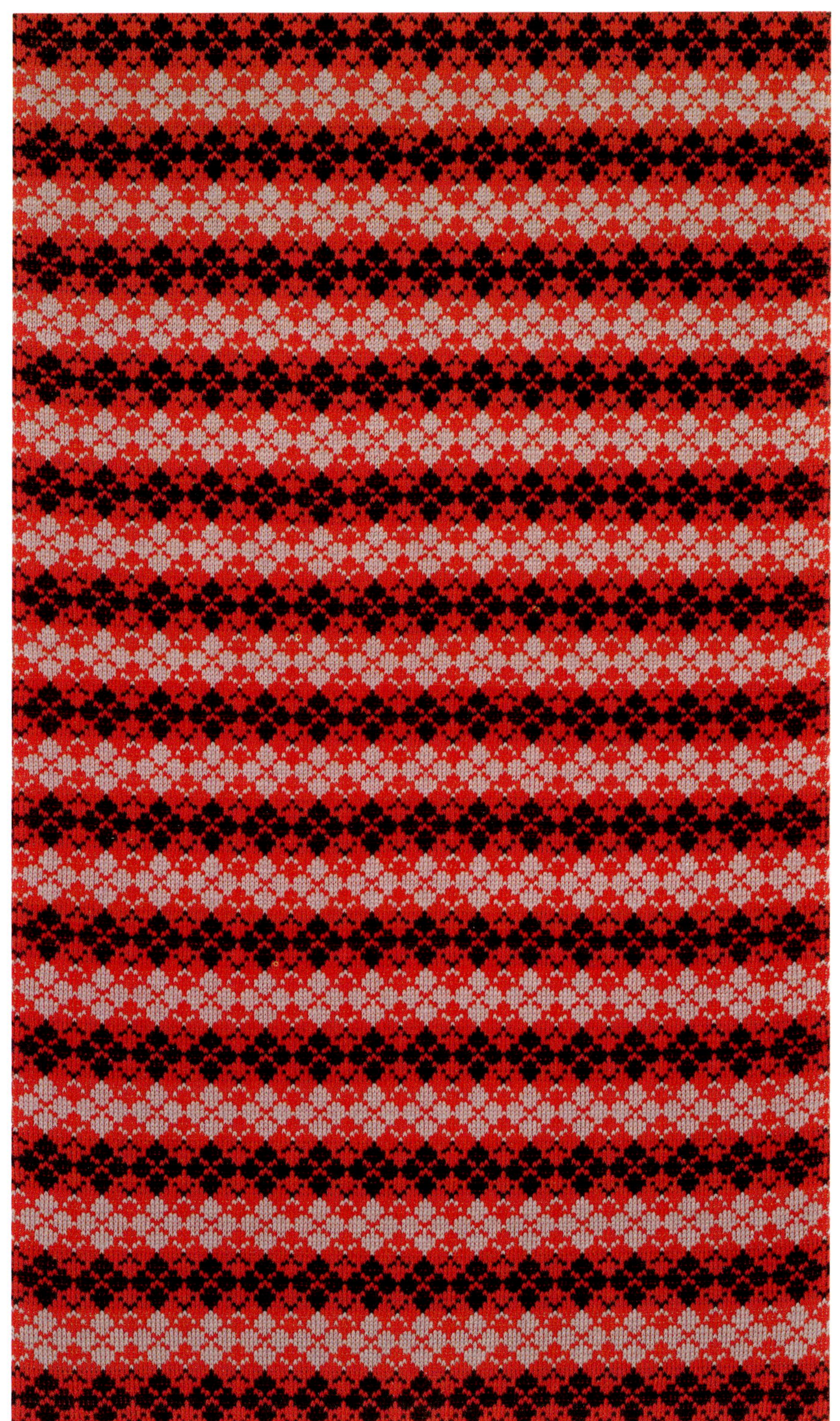

Checklist Height precedes width precedes depth

Richard Artschwager

Born: 1923, Washington, DC
Resides: New York, New York

Mirror, 1988
Formica and enamel on wood
30 3/8 × 24 3/8 × 3 7/8 inches
Courtesy Brooke Alexander Editions, New York

John Baldessari

Born: 1931, National City, California
Resides: Los Angeles, California

*A Two-Dimensional Surface Without Any
Articulation is a Dead Experience,* 1967
Acrylic on canvas
57 3/8 × 67 1/2 inches
Courtesy the artist

Ross Bleckner

Born: 1949, New York, New York
Resides: New York, New York

Gold Count No Count, 1991
Oil on canvas
96 × 72 inches
Collection United Yarn Products Company,
Arthur G. Rosen

Jonathan Borofsky

Born: 1942, Boston, Massachusetts
Resides: Los Angeles, California and New York,
New York

Untitled at 2,835,666 with *Chattering Man,* 1983
Untitled at 2,835,666 :
Ink and oil on paper
80 × 101 inches
Chattering Man:
Mixed media
80 × 23 × 13 inches
Courtesy Paula Cooper Gallery, New York

Daniel Buren

Born: 1938, Bouligne-Billancourt, France
Resides: Paris, France

Framed/Exploded/Defaced, 1979
Color aquatint etchings
25 fragments, individually framed
8 × 8 × 1/2 inches each, overall dimensions variable
Courtesy Crown Point Press, San Francisco

Peter Halley

Born: 1953, New York, New York
Resides: New York, New York

White Cell with Conduit, 1986
Day-Glo acrylic, acrylic and Roll•A•Tex on canvas
68 × 101 inches
Collection ZDS Trading, New York

303, 1991
Day-Glo acrylic, acrylic, and Roll•A•Tex on canvas
88 1/2 × 91 1/2 inches
Collection Cooperfund, Inc.

Mary Heilmann

Born: 1940, San Francisco, California
Resides: New York, New York

My Heart is a Flower, 1992
Oil on canvas
2 parts: (left) 42 × 42 inches; (right) 40 × 30 inches
71 × 61 inches overall
Courtesy Pat Hearn Gallery, New York

Peter Young, 1990
Oil on canvas
54 × 54 inches
Courtesy Pat Hearn Gallery, New York

Jasper Johns

Born: 1930, Augusta, Georgia
Resides: New York, New York

Corpse and Mirror, 1976
Lithograph
$30\frac{3}{4} \times 39\frac{5}{8}$ inches
©1995 Jasper Johns/VAGA, New York
Courtesy the artist and ULAE

Rachel Lachowicz

Born: 1964, San Francisco, California
Resides: New York, New York

Color Chart #4, 1992
From the series, *Eyeshadow*
Eyeshadow on aluminum
48 × 48 inches
Courtesy Shoshana Wayne Gallery, Santa Monica

Homage to Carl Andre, 1991/1994
Lipstick and wax
$\frac{3}{8} \times 72 \times 72$ inches
Courtesy the artist and
collection Newport Harbor Art Museum

Jonathan Lasker

Born: 1948, Jersey City, New Jersey
Resides: New York, New York

The Happiness of Cannibals, 1991
Oil on linen
$52\frac{1}{2} \times 63$ inches
Private collection, New York

Born Yesterday, 1989
Oil on linen
77 × 102 inches
Private collection, New York

Annette Lemieux

Born: 1957, Norfolk, Virginia
Resides: Brookline, Massachusetts

Black Mass, 1991
Mixed media
96 × 105 inches
Collection Emily Fisher Landau

Anonymity, 1992
Oil and gesso on canvas
72 × 66 inches
Courtesy the artist

Sherrie Levine

Born: 1947, Hazelton, Pennsylvania
Resides: New York, New York

Medium Check: 12, 1985
Casein and wax on mahogany
24 × 20 inches
Collection Carol and Arthur Goldberg

Untitled (Gold Knots: 5), 1987
Metallic paint on plywood
60 × 48 inches
Rubell Family Collections, Miami, Florida

Allan McCollum

Born: 1944, Los Angeles, California
Resides: New York, New York

10 Plaster Surrogates, 1982/92
Enamel on solid cast Hydrocal
10 parts, dimensions variable
24 × 168 inches overall
Courtesy John Weber Gallery, New York

Mark Milloff

Born: 1953, Miami, Florida
Resides: New York, New York

Untitled (Bars), 1993
Oil on canvas
48 × 30 inches
Collection Elizabeth and Steven Sobol

Fallen Target II, 1993
Wall piece: oil on canvas
36 × 36 inches
Floor piece: oil encased in shrink wrap
2 × 14 inches overall
Collection Sandra and James Leitner

Bruce Nauman

Born: 1941, Fort Wayne, Indiana
Resides: Galisteo, New Mexico

Ah Ha, 1975
One-color screenprint
$29\frac{1}{8} \times 41\frac{1}{8}$ inches
©1975 Gemini G.E.L.
Courtesy Gemini G.E.L., Los Angeles

Nam June Paik

Born: 1932, Seoul, Korea
Resides: New York, New York

Zen for TV, 1975–94
Video sculpture
$16 \times 12\frac{1}{2} \times 16$ inches
Courtesy Holly Solomon Gallery, New York

David Reed

Born: 1946, San Diego, California
Resides: New York , New York

No. 269, 1989
Oil and alkyd on linen
27 × 103 inches
Collection Judy and Harvey Gushner

No. 276, 1989
Oil and alkyd on linen
24 × 102 inches
Collection Barbara and Howard Morse

David Row

Born: 1954, Portland, Maine
Resides: New York, New York

Split Infinitive, 1990
Oil and wax on canvas
86 × 116 inches
Courtesy the artist and André Emmerich, New York

Untitled #99, 1990
Oil, wax, and charcoal, on wood and canvas
3 panels, 103 × 78 × 2 1/2 inches overall
Collection Livia and Marc Straus and
Melanie and Jeffrey Ambinder

Andres Serrano

Born: 1950, New York, New York
Resides: New York, New York

Circle of Blood, 1987
Cibachrome
40 × 60 inches, unframed
Courtesy Paula Cooper Gallery, New York

Milk, Blood, 1986
Cibachrome
40 × 60 inches, unframed
Courtesy Paula Cooper Gallery, New York

Rosemarie Trockel

Born: 1952, Schwerte, West Germany
Resides: Cologne, Germany

Untitled (plus-minus), 1985
Knitted wool
2 parts, 23 1/2 × 19 inches each
Courtesy Barbara Gladstone Gallery, New York

Untitled, 1987
Knitted wool
59 5/8 × 35 3/4 inches
Collection Raymond J. Learsy

A Debate on Abstraction. New York: The Bertha and Karl
Leubsdorf Art Gallery, Hunter College, 1988.

Barreres, Domingo et al. *The Image of Abstract Painting in the
80s* (exhibition catalogue). Waltham, MA: Rose Art
Museum, Brandeis University, 1990.

Bois, Yves-Alain. "Painting: The Task of Mourning." In
*Endgame: Reference and Simulation in Recent Painting and
Sculpture*, 29–49. Boston: Institute of Contemporary Art;
Cambridge, MA: MIT Press, 1986.

Cheng, Emily. *Abstraction/Abstraction* (exhibition catalogue).
Pittsburgh: Carnegie Mellon University Press, 1986.

Colpitt, Frances. "Abstraction at Eighty: Theory and
Experience of Painting." In Phyllis Plous and Frances
Colpitt, *Abstract Options*, 11–19. Santa Barbara, CA:
University Art Museum, 1988 (distributed by University of
Washington Press).

Conceptual Abstraction: November 7–December 21, 1991. New
York: Sidney Janis Gallery, 1991.

Contemporary Perspectives 1: Abstraction in Question. Sarasota,
FL: The John and Mabel Ringling Museum of Art, 1989.

Crone, Rainer and David Moos. "Painting in a Moment,
Painting at a Moment." In *Painting Alone*, 9–29. New York:
Pace Gallery, 1990.

Crow, Thomas. "The Return of Hank Herron." In *Endgame:
Reference and Simulation in Recent Painting and Sculpture*,
11–27. Boston: Institute of Contemporary Art; Cambridge,
MA: MIT Press, 1986.

Guilbaut, Serge. "Postwar Painting Games: The Rough and
the Slick." In *Reconstructing Modernism: Art in New York,
Paris, and Montreal, 1945–1964*, 30–84, edited by Serge
Guibaut. Cambridge, MA: MIT Press, 1990.

Hudspeth, Thomas. *Contemporary Abstract Painting* (exhibition
catalogue). Allentown, PA: Center for the Arts,
Muhlenberg College, 1983.

Kaufmann, Rita and Mike Metz. *Stubborn Painting: Now &
Then*. New York: Max Protetch Gallery, 1992.

Krauss, Rosalind. "Reading Jackson Pollock Abstractly." In
Rosalind Krauss, *The Originality of the Avant-Garde and*

B i b l i o g r a p h y

Other Modernist Myths, 221–42. Cambridge, MA: MIT Press, 1985.

Ostrow, Saul and Wolff Gallery. *Strategies for the Next Painting/Strategies for the Last Painting*. New York and Chicago: Wolff Gallery & Feigen Inc., 1990–91.

Plous, Phyllis. "The Conditioning of Our Time." In Phyllis Plous and Frances Colpitt, *Abstract Options*, 21–36. Santa Barbara, CA: University Art Museum, 1988 (distributed by University of Washington Press).

Sussman, Elisabeth. "The Last Picture Show." In *Endgame: Reference and Simulation in Recent Painting and Sculpture*, 51–69. Boston: Institute of Contemporary Art; Cambridge, MA: MIT Press, 1986.

PERIODICALS

"About the Sublime Today: A Conversation Between Peter Halley and Demetrio Paparoni." In *Tema Celeste International Art Magazine, Special Issue: The New Forms of Abstraction (Second Part)*, 34 (January–March 1992): 89.

Bochner, Mel. "Statement on Abstraction." In *Tema Celeste International Art Magazine, Special Issue: The New Forms of Abstraction (First Part)*, 32–33 (Autumn 1991): 86.

"David Row: A Conversation with Demetrio Paparoni." In *Tema Celeste International Art Magazine, Special Issue: The New Forms of Abstraction (Second Part)*, 34 (January–March 1992): 94–95.

Ellis, Stephen. "After the Fall." In *Tema Celeste International Art Magazine, Special Issue: The New Forms of Abstraction (Second Part)*, 34 (January–March 1992): 56–59.

Foster, Hal. "Signs Taken for Wonders." *Art in America* 74 (June 1986): 80–91.

Gilbert-Rolfe, Jeremy. "Abstract Painting and the Historical Object: Considerations on New Paintings by James Hayward." *Arts Magazine* 61 (April 1987): 30–36.

______. "The Current State of Nonrepresentation." *Visions* (Spring 1989): 3–7.

Haar, Michael. "The Meaning of Abstract Painting." In *Tema Celeste International Art Magazine, Special Issue: The New Forms of Abstraction (First Part)*, 32–33 (Autumn 1991): 86.

Halley, Peter. "Abstraction and Culture." In *Tema Celeste International Art Magazine, Special Issue: The New Forms of Abstraction (First Part)*, 32–33 (Autumn 1991): 57–60.

Kuspit, Donald. "Fin de Siècle Abstraction: The Ambiguous Return Inwards." In *Tema Celeste International Art Magazine, Special Issue: The New Forms of Abstraction (Second Part)*, 34 (January–March 1992): 56–59.

Madoff, Steven Henry. "The Return of Abstraction." *ARTnews* 85 (January 1986): 80–85.

McEvilley, Thomas. "Heads It's Form, Tails It's Not Content." *Artforum* 21/3 (November 1982): 50–61.

Mitchell, W. J. T. "Ut Pictura Theoria: Abstract Painting and Repression of Language."*Critical Inquiry* 15 (Winter 1989): 348–371.

Mosset, Olivier. "Deconstructing Abstraction." In *Tema Celeste International Art Magazine, Special Issue: The New Forms of Abstraction (First Part)*, 32–33 (Autumn 1991): 78.

Ostrow, Saul. "Strategies for a New Abstraction." In *Tema Celeste International Art Magazine, Special Issue: The New Forms of Abstraction (First Part)*, 32–33 (Autumn 1991): 66–71.

Paparoni, Demetrio. "The Orange and Its Juice." In *Tema Celeste International Art Magazine, Special Issue: The New Forms of Abstraction (First Part)*, 32–33 (Autumn 1991): 61–64.

Rand, Archie. "Concentric Collapse Awaiting Annealment." In *Tema Celeste International Art Magazine, Special Issue: The New Forms of Abstraction (Second Part)*, 34 (January–March 1992): 90.

Scully, Sean. "Abstraction is the Art of Our Time." In *Tema Celeste International Art Magazine, Special Issue: The New Forms of Abstraction (First Part)*, 32–33 (Autumn 1991), 77.

"Sean Scully: A Conversation with Demetrio Paparoni." In *Tema Celeste International Art Magazine, Special Issue: The New Forms of Abstraction (Third Part)*, 35 (April–May 1992), 82–83.

Steinberg, Leo and Donald Kuspit. "What Is the Meaning of…?" In *Tema Celeste International Art Magazine, Special Issue: The New Forms of Abstraction (First Part)*, 32–33 (Autumn 1991), 65.

Zinsser, John. "Geometry and Its Discontents." In *Tema Celeste International Art Magazine, Special Issue: The New Forms of Abstraction (First Part)*, 32–33 (Autumn 1991), 72–76.

© 1995 Independent Curators Incorporated
799 Broadway, Suite 205
New York, NY 10003
212-254-8200   Fax: 212-477-4781

Editor: Marybeth Sollins
Design and typography: Russell Hassell
Lithography: The Studley Press
Edition of 2500

Library of Congress Catalogue Card Number: 94-77787
ISBN: 0-916365-43-3